RACINE
Phèdre

E. D. JAMES

*Fellow of St John's College, Cambridge
and formerly Lecturer in French, University of Cambridge*

G. JONDORF

*Fellow of Girton College, Cambridge
and Lecturer in French, University of Cambridge*

CAMBRIDGE
UNIVERSITY PRESS

Published by the Press Syndicate of the University of Cambridge
The Pitt Building, Trumpington Street, Cambridge CB2 1RP
40 West 20th Street, New York, NY 10011–4211, USA
10 Stamford Road, Oakleigh, Melbourne 3166, Australia

First published 1994

Printed in Great Britain at the University Press, Cambridge

A catalogue record for this book is available from the British Library

Library of Congress cataloguing in publication data

James, E. D. (Edward D.)
Racine, Phèdre / E. D. James, G. Jondorf.
    p.   cm. – (Landmarks of world literature)
Includes bibliographical references.
ISBN 0 521 39319 1 (hardback).
ISBN 0 521 39721 9 (paperback)
1. Racine, Jean, 1639–1699. Phèdre.
2. Phaedra (Greek mythology) in literature.
I. Jondorf, Gillian. II. Title. III. Series.
PQ1898.J36 1994
842′.4–dc20 93-49361 CIP

ISBN 0 521 39319 1 hardback
ISBN 0 521 39721 9 paperback

Contents

v

Prefatory note

The text of *Phèdre* which we have used is that contained in the *Théâtre complet* of Racine, edited by J. Morel and A. Viala in the Classiques Garnier series (Paris, 1980). Readers using other editions will find very little variation in the text, but a good deal in the punctuation, which is largely a matter of editorial choice.

The task of composition has been shared as follows: Dr Jondorf has been responsible for the sections on Structure and Language, Dr James for the rest. We have, however, discussed and revised the whole work together.

Thanks for some helpful suggestions are due to the reader for the Cambridge University Press. Mrs Heather Henchie of the Cambridge University French Department is especially thanked for processing Dr James's manuscript.

E. D. J.
G. J.

Chronology

	Tragedy: writers and critics	*Cultural and historical events*
1562		Beginning of French Wars of Religion.
1570	Castelvetro, *Poetica d'Aristotele vulgarizzata.*	
1573	Garnier, *Hippolyte.*	
1589		Assassination of Henri III.
1593		Henri IV renounces Protestantism and enters Paris.
1598		Edict of Nantes. End of Wars of Religion.
1606	Pierre Corneille born.	
1607		Honoré d'Urfé, *L'Astrée*, t.1.
1610		Henri IV assassinated. Succeeded by Louis XIII, with Marie de Medici as regent. Honoré d'Urfé, *L'Astrée*, t.2.
1614		Majority of Louis XIII.
1615		Louis XIII marries Anne of Austria.
1619		Honoré d'Urfé, *L'Astrée*, t.3.
1622		Molière born.
1624		Richelieu *chef du conseil du roi.*
1627		Honoré d'Urfé, *L'Astrée*, t.4 and 5.
1630		Marie de Medici exiled.
1635	La Pinelière, *Hippolyte.*	Foundation of the Académie Française.
1637	P. Corneille, *Le Cid.* Rotrou, *Antigone.*	
1638	*Les Sentimens de l'Académie sur 'Le Cid'.*	Birth of the future Louis XIV.

1639	Jean Racine born.	
1640	P. Corneille, *Horace*.	C. Jansen, *Augustinus*.
1640–1	P. Corneille, *Cinna*.	
1642		Richelieu dies.
1642–3	P. Corneille, *Polyeucte*.	
1643		Louis XIII dies. Succeeded by Louis XIV. Regency of Anne of Austria. Mazarin first minister.
1644–5	P. Corneille, *Rodogune*.	
1644–50		La Calprenède, *Cassandre*, 10 vols.
1646	Gilbert, *Hippolyte*.	
1648		Treaty of Westphalia. End of Thirty Years War.
1648–9		Fronde parlementaire.
1649–53		Madeleine de Scudéry, *Artamène ou le grand Cyrus*, 10 vols.
1650–3		Fronde des Princes.
1651		Majority of Louis XIV.
1652	P. Corneille, *Pertharite*.	
1653		Condemnation of five propositions attributed to Jansen.
1654–60		Madeleine de Scudéry, *Clélie*, 10 vols.
1655	Racine attends school at the Granges of Port-Royal.	
1656	Th. Corneille, *Timocrate*.	
1656–7		Pascal, *Lettres provinciales*.
1657	D'Aubignac, *La Pratique du théâtre*.	
1658	Racine leaves Port-Royal for a year's Logic at the Collège d'Harcourt in Paris.	

Date		
1659	P. Corneille, *Œdipe*.	Peace of the Pyrenees. Louis XIV marries Maria Teresa, daughter of the King of Spain.
1660	P. Corneille, *Discours*.	Louis XIV assumes personal reign.
after 1660	Racine translates parts of Aristotle's *Poetics*.	
1661		Mazarin dies.
1664	Quinault, *Astrate, roi de Tyr*. Racine, *La Thébaïde*.	Molière, *Le Tartuffe*, first version.
1665	Racine, *Alexandre le Grand*.	La Rochefoucauld, *Maximes* (first edition). Molière, *Dom Juan*.
1666		Molière, *Le Misanthrope*.
1666–7	Racine quarrels with Port-Royal over the denunciation of the writings of novelists and playwrights by P. Nicole in *Les Visionnaires*.	
1667	Racine, *Andromaque*.	P. Nicole, *Traité de la comédie*.
1668		'Peace of the Church' with Jansenists begins.
1669	Racine, *Britannicus*.	
1670	Racine, *Bérénice*.	Pascal, *Pensées*.
1672	Racine, *Bajazet*. Quinault, *Bellérophon*. Th. Corneille, *Ariane*.	Louis XIV wages war on the Dutch.
1673	Racine received into the Académie Française.	Molière dies.
1674	Racine, *Mithridate*. Racine, *Iphigénie*. P. Corneille, *Suréna*.	Boileau, *L'Art poétique*.
1675	Bidar, *Hippolyte*. Pradon, *Tamerlan*. Quinault, *Thésée* (music by Lully).	

1677	Racine, *Phèdre*. Pradon, *Phèdre et Hippolyte*. Subligny, *Dissertation sur les tragédies de 'Phèdre et Hippolyte'*. Racine appointed (with Boileau) Historiographer Royal.	
1679		La Rochefoucauld, *Maximes*, fifth and definitive edition. Madame de Lafayette, *La Princesse de Clèves*.
1678		Peace of Nijmegen. Persecution of Jansenists resumes.
1682		P. Bayle, *Pensées diverses sur la comète*, speculates on the relation between beliefs and moral conduct.
1683	Racine in Alsace with King and army.	
1684	Corneille dies.	
1685		Revocation of Edict of Nantes.
1688		War of the League of Augsburg begins.
1689	Racine, *Esther*.	
1691	Racine, *Athalie* (private performance).	
1697		War of the League of Augsburg ends. Treaty of Rijswijck. P. Bayle, *Dictionnaire historique et critique*.
1699	Racine dies in Paris.	
1707	Edmund [Neale] Smith, *Phaedra and Hippolitus*.	
1712	Ambrose Philips, *The Distrest Wife*.	

Year		
1713		Treaty of Utrecht.
1714		Fénelon, *Lettre à l'Académie*.
1715		Louis XIV dies. Succeeded by Louis XV. Regency of Philippe d'Orléans begins.
1716	Racine, *Athalie* (public performance).	
1723		Majority of Louis XV.
1731		Prévost, *Histoire du chevalier Des Grieux et de Manon Lescaut*.
1733	J.-Ph. Rameau, *Hippolyte et Aricie*, libretto by Pellegrin.	

Chapter 1

The context of *Phèdre*

Introduction: versions of a legend

Phèdre represents the culmination of seventeenth-century French classical tragedy and can be fully understood only against the background of seventeenth-century French political, social, and literary history, of which we provide a brief sketch. It should not be supposed, however, that some evolutionary process was at work from which Racine's greatest tragedy emerged by an inherent logic. It is the highly individual work of an original genius, a play organically related to his previous plays, but not their inevitable outcome, and still less that of the creations of his French predecessors who, like himself, were indebted to Seneca and, indirectly at least, to Euripides.

Euripides' *Hippolytus* (429 BC) is the story of the revenge of Aphrodite, goddess of love, on Hippolytus for neglecting her in favour of Artemis, goddess of chastity. Hippolytus is the son of Theseus and stepson of Phaedra, Theseus' second wife. While Theseus is away, Phaedra falls in love with Hippolytus, and her nurse reveals her feelings to him. He rejects her advances. Phaedra hangs herself, leaving tablets denouncing Hippolytus as her seducer. Theseus banishes Hippolytus and calls upon Poseidon to punish him. A monstrous bull sent from the sea terrifies his horses and he is dragged to his death. Theseus learns belatedly of his misjudgement from Artemis. In a final exchange with his dying son, Theseus is forgiven by him.

In the *Phaedra* (*c.* AD 50) of Seneca, it is Phaedra herself who reveals her love to Hippolytus, seizes his sword, which he drops after threatening to kill her, and produces it in evidence when she accuses him of assault. When Hippolytus has died a

1

violent death following his father's curse, Phaedra confesses her guilt and commits suicide in despair. Apart from Neptune, the gods have no role in the play, which has become a drama of human passion.

In his *Phèdre* (1677), Racine adapts the ancient tale to contemporary French taste with immense skill and to powerful effect. The austerely celibate Hippolytus of myth is transformed into a young lover, the object of his affections being the partially invented figure of Aricie, offspring of an enemy dynasty and potential pretender to the throne of Athens. Phèdre's anguished love for Hippolyte, which Venus has inflicted upon her, is exacerbated by intense jealousy when she learns that he loves another. She does not herself accuse Hippolyte of rape, but does acquiesce in Œnone's resolve to do so. Filled with remorse, she takes a lethal poison, only to be utterly consumed by her sense of guilt on learning of the destruction of Hippolyte by a sea-monster, and dies in despair and self-loathing.

Four or five predecessors of Racine composed plays on the theme of Phaedra's love for her stepson Hippolytus, but they mostly followed Seneca too closely to have had much to offer which was not already present in the Latin dramatist. Only the *Hippolyte* (1573) of the gifted sixteenth-century dramatist Robert Garnier may give some foretaste of the poetry of Racine's tragedy. The *Bellérophon* (1672) of Philippe Quinault, on the love of Stheneboea, wife of the king of Argos, for the eponymous hero, introduces a rival for his love, as does the *Hippolyte* (1675) of Bidar, and Racine may well have owed something to the *Ariane* (1672) of Thomas Corneille, which depicts Phèdre's jealousy of her sister. But all the seventeenth-century predecessors of Racine flinch from depicting an incestuous relationship, and Phèdre and Thésée are represented as fiancés, not as man and wife. In Gilbert's play of 1646, Hippolyte is even shown in love with Phèdre. Needless to say, such adaptations of the legend deprive it of the sense of tragic guilt which gives Racine's play its special force.

Racinian tragedy reflects the somewhat oppressive and enclosed atmosphere of the salon and court culture of his time, disillusioned concerning human ideals, generating its own self-destructive passions, and inclined to a fatalistic pessimism not uncongenial to an autocratic political regime. It was an age, also, when cracks were about to appear in the triumphal façade of apparently timeless classical values. To have captured the grandeur and the self-doubts of high classicism in a play on a Euripidean mythological theme, enriched by Senecan moral insight and by the poetry of Virgil and Ovid, yet creating a majestic poetry of its own, is a unique achievement, for the society and the ethos from which it emerged were on the brink – or in the process – of change into something like our own bourgeois-utilitarian world in which high tragedy is remote from our experience, relegated, in fact, to the realm of literary artifice. Yet Racine's allegory of the struggle of conscience and desire retains its power to awaken echoes in our own sensibility and has continued in succeeding generations to stimulate creative minds throughout Europe to refashion in their turn, and in the image of their own obsessions and anxieties, Racine's transmutation of an ancient theme.

Politics, society, and drama in seventeenth-century France

The appearance of monumental grandeur and simplicity which attaches to the age of Louis XIV during which Racine wrote all his plays must be set against a historical background of political and social disorder. The reign of the cardinal de Richelieu as chief counsellor to Marie de Medici and Louis XIII, which saw the founding of the French Academy and coincided very largely with the creation of Pierre Corneille's most original or most powerful plays, was a period of turbulence and at first of conspiracies and rebellions. Rebellions among the nobility were severely repressed and their powers as provincial governors were restricted by the presence of the state administrative officers known as *intendants*. The conspiracies of unruly nobles and their conflicts with their rulers which Corneille depicts in his great tragedies of the thirties and forties can be seen as reflecting in a stylised way the realities of that age.

The last and decisively disastrous attempt of the nobles to assert their independence, however, came with the civil wars known as the Frondes in the late 1640s and early 1650s, at the time of the Regency of Anne of Austria and under the young King Louis XIV and his minister Mazarin. The collapse of the Frondes marked the end of any serious threat to the authority of the central administration and heralded an age of systematic reduction of the nobility to political impotence by a determinedly autocratic ruler who never forgot the humiliation inflicted on him in early adolescence by the Frondes. In 1660, Louis inaugurated his personal reign, and Mazarin died the year after. Louis was to pursue a repressive policy within and a policy of wars of expansion without. The Jansenist community of Port-Royal by which Racine had been educated, but which the King suspected of having supported the Frondes, was brought under central control in 1661, and an uneasy 'Peace of the Church' with the Jansenists prevailed from 1668 to 1679, coinciding with the middle years of Racine's dramatic career. Abroad, Louis waged war against Holland, and if he did not achieve the crushing victory that he had intended, he secured French frontiers to north and east by treaties of 1678 and 1679, and demonstrated the dominant role of France in Europe. At the same time he succeeded in imposing on opinion inside and outside France an image of French political and cultural superiority and prestige.

If the heroic dramas of Corneille with their ancient or legendary settings reflected the conflicts of interest and principle which lay behind the political struggles of the the 1640s, the heroic novel of the time, modelled on the ancient epic, depicted the martial and amorous exploits of the heroes of antiquity adapted to a modern taste and resembling or presaging the romantic posturings of the aristocratic *frondeurs*. But a transition is evident in the long novels of the *précieuse* Madeleine de Scudéry, published in the 1650s, which, from a romanticised and sentimentalised depiction of ancient heroes in *Artamène, ou Le grand Cyrus*, pass in *Clélie* to an evocation, still under ancient names, of the conversations and discussions of those who frequented her salon. The preoccupation of

Mademoiselle de Scudéry, and of the preciosity which she favoured, with the emancipation of women and with their emotional life made a deep impression on the literature of the age of high classicism in France. Even Corneille, who had seemed to lose his touch with his miserably unsuccessful tragedy *Pertharite* (1652) on an episode from the history of the Goths, returned to the stage in 1659 with his *Œdipe*, adding love interest by way of a secondary plot which overshadows the great tragic theme bequeathed by Sophocles.

Audiences in the age of high classicism were above all concerned to be entertained. Romance and gallantry figured largely in the plays of Philippe Quinault in the 1660s and 1670s, which were pervaded by sensibility: even 'I hate you' being said tenderly, as Boileau ironically observed. But Quinault acquired particularly a reputation as a librettist for the operas of Lully, many of which had mythological plots. These too were essentially for entertainment and spectacle. Scenery and machinery were especially appreciated. The vogue of sensibility and taste for lavish entertainment and spectacle were congenial to an autocratic regime which sought to encourage the creation of a culture of brilliance and prestige, and preferred to have the nobility harmlessly occupied at court rather than plotting in their domains. On the other hand, their confined existence, with its intrigues, frustrations, and suppressed emotional violence, created a climate of disillusion akin to that evoked in Madame de La Fayette's ostensibly historical novel, *La Princesse de Clèves* (1675). To this climate of disillusion, the religious pessimism of writers within and without the Jansenist fold made its own contribution. The tragedies of Racine, however, apart from the two late plays, *Esther* and *Athalie*, are essentially pagan in character and in any case problematic rather than doctrinaire.

The conditions under which French classical drama was normally staged were restrictive. Plays were performed in converted indoor tennis-courts or, more rarely, in theatres built on the same plan as these. The chief Paris theatre for the performance of tragedy, the Hôtel de Bourgogne, where Racine's major secular plays were staged, was such a theatre, purpose-built in 1548. The rectangular structure of the tennis-court or theatre afforded only limited visibility to the specta-tors. These sat along the sides of the court, opposite one another rather than facing the raised stage, or stood massed in the pit (*parterre*), where vision largely depended on one's being able to see between, or over the heads of, others. Privi-leged spectators sat on the stage itself, and, besides inconven-iencing actors, were themselves too close to the action to follow it with ease. Costumes were rich, an amalgam of ancient and contemporary French dress, but scenery was simple, making use of standard sets, the indication 'palais à volonté' meaning any available scenery representing a palace. Racine, however, seems to have prescribed more precise set-tings for his plays, as, for instance, the vaulted palace of *Phèdre* (line 854). Lighting was by fitful candle-flames, which may have lent themselves to lighting effects of sorts but must also have made recognition of facial expression and body language difficult. In fact, the visual appeal in Racine is made more widely to the mind's eye and to the imagination through the medium of language. For the delivery of the lines, Racine seems to have favoured a moderately rhetorical style of decla-mation, exploiting variation of vocal pitch and loudness for dramatic effect. (See D. Maskell, *Racine. A Theatrical Reading* (Oxford, 1991), pp. 9–125.)

Principles of French classical tragedy

French classical dramatic theory is deeply indebted to the interpretation of Aristotle's *Poetics* by Renaissance scholars. The publication in 1498 of Giorgio Valla's Latin translation of that work prompted a whole series of editions, translations, and commentaries, of which Lodovico Castelvetro's *Poetica d'Aristotele vulgarizzata e sposta* (*Aristotle's Poetics Vernacu-larized and Expounded*) of 1570 is among the most notable. Castelvetro argues that his predecessors in translating the *Poetics* had not realised that Aristotle's work was a rough draft for a two-volume treatise. He proposed, therefore, to expand and enlarge the *Poetics* so as to make of it a substitute for Aristotle's lost treatise. The resulting work is probably twenty times the length of Aristotle's brief and incomplete outline. Castelvetro, who is not a faithful follower of Aristotle and does not hesitate to distort or reject his views, is the chief source of the French classical doctrine of the three unities of action, time, and place (a single action in a single place and lasting no more than a single day), a fact which is not without irony, since Castelvetro appears to have favoured realism in the theatre, whereas the unities have come to be seen as the height of artifice. Nevertheless, Castelvetro saw them as closer to reality than settings requiring the audience to transport themselves in time and space.

Racine's great seventeenth-century predecessor Pierre Corneille, who was born in 1606, was writing for the theatre before the classical rules were well established in France, but his early plays, apart from the first, belong to the 1630s, the period when the debate over the rules was at its height. While soon showing himself to be largely in tune with classical conceptions of dramatic technique, he also displayed a great independence of mind, equal to that of Castelvetro, to whom he was indebted, as well as the creative imagination to impose his own artistic vision on the drama of his age. The performance of Corneille's *Le Cid* in 1637 prompted the French Academy's critique (*Les Sentiments de l'Académie sur 'Le Cid'*, 1638) which spurred Corneille to closer conformity to classical conventions.

Corneille's finest tragedies belong chiefly to the first half of the century. As a playwright of established reputation he published in 1660 three *Discours* on the principles of drama. It seems likely that he was at least in part concerned to reply to *La Pratique du théâtre* (1657, but written perhaps in the 1640s) of the Abbé d'Aubignac, an influential work of theory and practice. D'Aubignac championed the principle of verisimilitude in the theatre, and is also notable for his insistence that the unities are not simply decreed by authority but are founded in reason – a major reason being their contribution to verisimilitude. Corneille's *Discours* are in fact concerned with the two questions of whether a play has to be morally useful and whether it has to be probable or plausible.

Inevitably, Corneille quotes Aristotle's prescription for the tragic hero, requiring that he should not be wholly virtuous, since the downfall of such a man would provoke moral indignation, nor wholly evil, for that downfall would then be his just desert. But Corneille disagrees with Aristotle, pointing to heroes or heroines of his own plays who are successful tragic figures in spite of being examples of types of which Aristotle disapproves.

In his discussion of the sources of tragic feeling, Corneille concerns himself with the question of whether, or how far, it is permissible to change anything in subjects taken from legend or history. He quotes Aristotle as saying that traditional subjects should not be altered and that Clytemnestra should not be killed by anyone other than her son Orestes, and so on. On this Corneille comments that while the traditional *outcome* of the story must be maintained, the way in which the outcome is arrived at is open to modification. He cites the different ways in which the death of Clytemnestra was treated by Sophocles and Euripides. It is at once obvious that Racine could offer the same justification for his own treatment of the Hippolytus legend. But whereas Corneille seeks tragic subjects in attested extraordinary characters and incidents, French classical principles, and Racine following them, require conformity to the demands of 'vraisemblance'. This will cause problems for Racine himself when he turns to myth for tragic themes.

On the unities we need note only two remarks on those of time and place. Corneille asserts that the unity of time is necessary on the grounds of realism, but that the exact duration of the action need not be indicated if probability is somewhat forced. Of the unity of place, he remarks that if it is unavoidable to have the action in more than one place, then these places should not have need of different scenery and in no circumstances should they be named, only the general location in which they are contained. What Corneille is proposing is a unity of place achieved by an illusion. The action is to take place in a single but undefined location. It is a single location but represents or may represent a plurality of its kind. Corneille operates with a much more restricted form of illusion than does Shakespeare, whose plays range over a variety of imagined historical settings. On the other hand, although French classical principles may confine the characters physically in a conventional room or palace, they impose no restrictions on the minds or imaginations of the characters, which may wander far and wide in space and time.

Corneille's plays and theoretical writings offer important models for Racine to imitate or reject. Racine was exceptional, however, in having a competent knowledge of Greek and in his direct study of Greek tragedies, on which he has left some notes, and of Aristotle's *Poetics*, of which he translated certain portions. These last give a clue to the direction of his interests, although the date of their writing is uncertain. It no doubt lies between that of the *Discours* (1660) of Corneille and that of his own *Phèdre* (1677). No less interesting, but quite different in character, are the prefaces to his plays, which, as was common in seventeenth-century France, were apologetic in character, defending his plays against not always well-intentioned criticism, or passing over to attack on his critics. He was particularly exposed to accusations of infringement, real or imaginary, of classical rules or conventions, and vigorously asserted the conformity of his practice to that favoured by critical authorities – notably Aristotle.

The first of Racine's prefaces, that to his second play, *Alexandre le Grand* (1665), reveals the areas in which a playwright might be exposed to critical attack. Racine insists on the technical orthodoxy of his play: all his scenes are well filled, they are firmly and coherently linked to one another, no actor comes on stage without the reason for his appearance being clearly indicated. More significantly for his own individual mode of writing, he claims to have kept his critics interested, perhaps in spite of themselves, from beginning to end of a play containing few incidents and little matter.

This already points to the 'inwardness' of the Racinian play – the concentration on psychological conflict rather than on physical action and events. The conception culminates in *Bérénice* (1670) in the preface to which Racine observes that invention consists in making something out of nothing. The contrary view, which attaches value to multiplicity of incident, offends against the principle of 'vraisemblance', since the unity of time does not admit of the occurrence of many events in the restricted time of the action of the play. This is surely directed against Corneille or his supporters, and Racine taunts dramatists who fill their plays with incident with lacking the fertility and the power to keep the interest of the audience during five acts through an action which is simple, sustained by the power of the passions, the beauty of the sentiments, and the elegance of the expression. There is a significant difference here from the concerns or at any rate the characteristics of the Cornelian play, which is marked rather by energy and epi-grammatic force of expression, loftiness of sentiments, and imperiousness of personalities.

Already in the preface to *Alexandre le Grand* Racine is wrangling with the critics over his portrayal of his heroes: Taxile, they say, lacks integrity – or he is unjustly treated; Alexandre is too amorous – or he is insufficiently amorous. This is not merely Racine's use of the familiar polemical device of setting critics against one another, it reveals disagreement over the moral concerns of literary works and over the role of the love interest in serious drama. In the prefaces to *Andromaque* (1667), a play evocative of the Trojan War and its after-math, Racine answers critics of his depiction of his protagon-ists by declaring stoutly that they are so famous in antiquity that he could not change their characters. If he has toned down the ferocity of Pyrrhus a little, he cannot make of him an amorous hero after the manner of seventeenth-century roman-ces, which, Racine remarks ironically, Pyrrhus had not read. As he will continue to do thereafter, Racine draws attention to Aristotle's principle that tragic characters should not be entirely good nor entirely evil, but should display a middling goodness of character, that is to say a virtue capable of weakness, and that they should fall into misfortune by some error of conduct which elicits compassion rather than abhor-rence. In his Preface to *Phèdre*, Racine applies the principle not only to the heroine, but also to Hippolyte, whose failing is said to be his involuntary passion for Aricie, the daughter and sister of mortal enemies of Hippolyte's father.

Racine's translations of parts of the *Poetics* of Aristotle are interesting for the topics selected. Racine appears to be particularly preoccupied with character, psychology, and the tragic emotion. It would be a mistake to conclude from this that he is uninterested in the technicalities of playwriting, for these were much more minutely prescribed by contemporary theorists than by Aristotle. Nor can Racine be held to be unconcerned with plot, and if he prizes simplicity, it is in contrast to his French predecessors and contemporaries rather than to the Greeks. It could even be claimed that an interest in character, psychology, and emotional drama does not distinguish him from Corneille. What does distinguish him is an affinity with Aristotle's conception of these, where Corneille and Castelvetro before him had frankly demurred. Corneille's characters are concerned with their 'image', with asserting their personalities, whatever weaknesses may lie behind the façade. Racine's characters are drawn back on themselves by their inner tensions. For Racine, the Aristotelian characterisation of the hero as a man of middling goodness of character has a special significance as allowing for ambiguity or inner conflict – admittedly not Aristotle's concern, which was rather with the aesthetico-moral acceptability of such a character's tragic fate.

In his conception of tragic catharsis, Racine is certainly closer to Aristotle than are his predecessors. Whereas Castelvetro thought the concept a utilitarian irrelevance and Corneille thought it unintelligible, Racine affirmed the principle of purging emotional excess which lay behind it. But if Aristotle's conception was based on a medical conception of purgation and healing, Racine's is more moral in character, aiming at promoting moderation, reason, and balance in our emotional life. In attributing a moral utility to tragedy, Racine concurs with the critical orthodoxy of his time. His conception is part of a tragic sense which is absent or less marked in Corneille, whose dominant concern appears to be that of theatrical impact.

As Vinaver has pointed out (*Racine et la poésie tragique*, Paris, 1951, pp. 182–6), the Aristotelian concept of 'anagnorisis' ('recognition', 'discovery') attracts Racine's special attention, but is also modified (rather, perhaps, than misunderstood). Aristotle's 'anagnorisis' is the protagonist's recognition of the victim of his/her misdeed, as, most strikingly, in the case of Sophocles' Œdipus. To judge by his translations from the *Poetics*, Racine's 'reconnaissance' is recognition not of the identity of a victim, but of the horror of what the perpetrator has done. The notion that the downfall of the hero or heroine might be due simply to an error or false step ('hamartia') was not acceptable to the seventeenth-century French critical mind, not at any rate to Racine's. Consequently, while the downfall of the tragic hero or heroine cannot be a result of deliberate wickedness or vice if he or she is to be pitied, it is nevertheless the result of a 'faute' or misdemeanour (although neither the French or Greek term is closely defined). In fact, in Racine's plays, as distinct from his translation of the *Poetics*, the hero or heroine suffers rather from a failing, 'défaut', or 'faiblesse'. For what brings about the downfall of the Racinian tragic figure is not so much a particular misdemeanour, as an egoistic ruling passion which he or she cannot control. But the plays contain images of innocence and purity. The most egoistic characters may reveal a nostalgia for innocence, and often have moments or periods of insight into the destructiveness of their passions, but the nostalgia and the lucidity serve only to heighten their sense and our sense of their helplessness to escape from themselves or their predicament.

A Racinian leitmotiv: the 'coupable innocent'

Racine's theatre continues the vogue of love and politics which characterises the work of his predecessors, but conveys a more powerful sense of his characters' inner tragedy. His tragic protagonists, several of whom are taken from myth or legend, are victims of temperament or circumstance, of fate or of divine displeasure, and among them are figures foreshadowing Phèdre, the 'coupable innocente', characters who feel themselves guilty when they are not, or whose responsibility for their actions is open to question. Racine plainly has a particular interest in such morally problematic characters.

Racine's first extant play, *La Thébaïde* (1664), is Greek legend at one or more removes. It is chiefly indebted to the *Antigone* (1637) of his gifted French predecessor Jean Rotrou, and to the dramatic scenes composed by Seneca under the title *Phoenissae* (*The Phoenician Maidens*). Both Rotrou and Seneca are indebted to the *Phoenissae* of Euripides, but Racine's claim in the preface to *La Thébaïde*, written eleven years after the play, that he himself drew on Euripides, is a deception designed to enhance the status of his own play. Rotrou's *Antigone* combines the story of the sons of Œdipus and Jocasta and of their sister Antigone. The principle of the unity of action required the rejection of one or other of the two actions, and that of Antigone was rejected by Racine in favour of the story of the enmity of the brothers Eteocles and Polynices. Racine develops the love interest and the role of Creon, the villain of the piece, who himself becomes a rival in love. But the value of the play lies not in these elements of gallantry but in the powerful central theme: the pathological hatred of the two brothers and their confrontation with the impressive figure of their mother Jocasta. Racine puts great emphasis on the family history and the persecution of the gods. By taking the Œdipus legend at a later stage than does Corneille in his *Œdipe* (1659) Racine is able to make use of the background of incest and horror when presenting the blood feud of Œdipus' sons. The strong emphasis on the ineluctability of fate is in marked contrast to Corneille's affirmation of free will in his *Œdipe* and offers a clear example of a change in the moral climate of drama. It is at all events of interest that Racine's first extant play should have taken as its subject a Greek tragic theme and treated it without any mitigation of its essential brutality and horror.

The gods are present in Racine's play through the pronouncement of the oracle, which declares that the Theban war will cease only with the death of the last in the royal line. The audience can have had no difficulty in interpreting this to mean the destruction of the royal line in its entirety. Jocaste proclaims from the outset the accursed destiny of the 'race of Laius' (her first husband), and although the gods are implored by Antigone and herself to spare the family, these pleas are despairing. Polynice speaks of the injustice of the gods, and Jocaste's complaint fills a whole scene in which she herself figures as a notable 'coupable innocente':

JOCASTE
Will these dire torments last for ever?
Will they never exhaust the vengeance of the gods?
Will they cause me to suffer so many cruel deaths
Without ever hastening me into the grave?
O heaven, how much less fearful would your rigours be
If the thunderbolt overwhelmed the guilty straight away!
And how infinite your chastisements seem
When you allow those you punish to live!
You know full well that since that shameful day
When I found myself wife of my own son,
The least of the torments suffered by my heart
Is as great as all the pains of hell.
And yet, O Gods, should an involuntary crime
Have brought upon itself all your wrath?
Alas! Did I recognise my luckless son?
You yourself drew him into my arms.
You it was whose rigour opened that precipice before me.
Such is the supreme justice of the mighty gods!
To the brink of crime they lead our steps;
They cause us to commit it, then brook no excuse!
Do they then take pleasure in making criminals
In order to make of them illustrious wretches?
And can they not, when filled with wrath,
Seek criminals to whom their crime is sweet?   (III.ii.591)

While the curse which hangs over the house of Laius is powerfully evoked, its working out is displayed as the effect of the ambitions and personalities of the characters. The oracle figures rather as a forecast than as the expression of an immutable decree of the gods. This disjunction – and linkage – between the human and divine in the motivation of the characters is to recur in those of Racine's plays which have a mythological content.

In *Andromaque* (1667) Racine combines more successfully the persuasive power of Greek legend and the compelling force of love and passion. But Greek legend remains at a remove. Racine indeed quotes as source only a short passage from Virgil's *Aeneid*. Seneca's *Troades* (*The Trojan Women*), based largely on Euripides' work of the same name, is another source. But legend figures as a backdrop to the action, and is vividly remembered by the characters for whom it was a disastrous or exciting experience. In this way, characters take on that larger-than-life appearance which is the prerogative of the figure of legend defined as she or he usually is by some characteristic trait. Thus Pyrrhus is the ruthless but charming conqueror, Hermione the jealous fury, Andromaque the dutiful widow and mother, Oreste the character dogged by fate. Oreste is the sole truly mythological figure in the play, however, and clearly has an important role, both structurally – since the play begins with mention of his melancholy destiny and ends with his madness – and in the creation of the play's tragic pathos. In his madness, Oreste has a vision of the Furies, and even if one explains this as a hallucination one must ask why he has this strange sense of persecution and guilt. Clearly it is integral to the character *qua* tragic, the figure of the 'coupable innocent', the innocently guilty, of which Phèdre is to be the most powerful example in Racine. What is interesting is that another explanation of Oreste's madness is given as the capriciousness with which he has been treated by Hermione. If this is the explanation, then the vision of the Furies is a symptom of the madness rather than a cause, but the mythical quality of the experience remains despite the obligation which Racine undoubtedly feels to offer a more rational – or more 'vraisemblable' – explanation as well as the mythical.

Henceforth, however, and remarkably, myth disappears from Racinian tragedy until *Iphigénie* (1674). Nevertheless, the savage emotions which bind and repel rebellious son and dominating mother in the Roman play *Britannicus* (1669), the picture of ruthlessness inherited, and ruthlessness encouraged by maternal example, offer at least some analogy or continuity with the family curse of Greek legend or myth. Great interest attaches to Racine's depiction of Néron as a 'nascent monster', goaded to evil by the egocentric and domineering personality of his mother and by his evil genius Narcisse, but hesitating under the moderating influence of the staid counsellor Burrhus. This is a study not simply of an evil personality, but of how Néron came to do the evil that he might not have done. The play clearly raises questions about the extent of Néron's culpability for his actions.

The problem of culpability arises in a different way in *Bajazet* (1672), a tragedy set in a seraglio, over which the order of the absent Sultan hangs like a decree of fate. The Sultana Roxane is a figure of primitive passion within a regal personality, but her rival for Bajazet's love, the gentler Atalide, strikes a new note of self-reproach. In the final speech of the play Atalide, who has persuaded her lover Bajazet to pretend to be in love with the Sultana and has then become jealous of her, blames herself for the death of her lover when the truth is discovered:

> At last, the end has come; and by my trickery,
> Unfair suspicions, fatal caprices,
> I have arrived at the painful moment when
> I see my lover dying of my crime!   (V.xii.1722)

The tragic pathos is a moral pathos attaching once again to the innocently guilty figure, for Atalide's doubts and fears about Bajazet's fidelity have been entirely understandable and, at worst, misguided. Applying an Aristotelian principle, we might see her as having made a false step. That she is tortured by remorse and sees herself as a moral criminal reveals her to be sister to the anguished figure of Phèdre.

With *Iphigénie* (1674), indebted to the *Iphigenia at Aulis* of Euripides, Racine is for the first time inspired directly by Greek tragedy. Agamemnon, the commander of the becalmed Greek fleet, having offended Diane (Artemis) finds himself told by an oracle to sacrifice his daughter Iphigénie if the gods are to relent and allow the winds to blow again, to bear the Greek fleet to Troy. His moral dilemma forms the dramatic centre of the play. Agamemnon is compelled to react to the oracle and to make painful choices. He must choose between the demands made on him by his responsibilities as commander of an army, by the promptings of his own amour-propre, by his concern for the feelings of his formidable wife Clytemnestre, and by his deep affection for his daughter. The oracle initiates a struggle of conscience in which Agamemnon takes on the central role of the figure at once culpable and innocent, one whose moral character is problematic. The moral force of the characterisation is unmistakable, but it does not have the supernatural dimension of the character of Phèdre. In Agamemnon, the guilt resides in the character's pride and egoism, sorely put to the test by the gods' ironic demand that he should sacrifice his beloved daughter and so, in effect, preserve his glory at the expense of the being he holds most dear. The moral failing is his own, the role of the gods is to give it destructive potential. In Phèdre, the failing itself is divinely inspired and felt as alien. For Phèdre, possession by Venus is akin to rape and induces a comparable self-loathing. The crime is the doing of a goddess but the sense of guilt is her own.

The Racinian tragic hero(ine), neither wholly good nor wholly evil, is often a victim of the gods who have the power to undermine from within. The formula extends even to Athalie, Racine's last great heroine, yet the play of that name (first acted privately in 1691) is an apologetic work designed to celebrate the victory of the god of righteous vengeance over his enemies. Athalie, a worshipper of Baal, has a criminal past, but she is encountered at a time when she has been conducting herself humanely. She is demoralised by bad dreams and undermined by her own sensibility, drawn instinctively as she is to the young Eliacin, who is in reality her grandson Joas, future King of the Jews, whose royal dynasty Athalie has vowed to exterminate. Our sense of her criminality is moderated by our awareness of her human feelings. Because the battle between the once great queen and the almighty God of the Jews is so unequal, the Jewish God seems as vindictive as the gods of the Greeks, and Athalie is seen as a tragic victim like the hero(in)es of Racine's earlier plays. The well-tried tragic formula undermines the apologetic message. By 1716 when the play was first publicly performed, the climate of opinion was changing, and to the devotees of the Enlightenment the intended message would come to seem one of superstition and fanaticism. They were reduced to admiring the form and style of the play while finding its message tedious. Many modern readers appear to be in the same predicament. *Phèdre*, proposing no clear message, speaks more convincingly to our age of moral uncertainty.

Chapter 2

Phèdre, the play

Structure

The structure of *Phèdre*, as of any regular play of the French
seventeenth century, could be described in the terminology of
contemporary theorists. Thus Théramène in I.i is serving as
what Corneille calls a 'personnage protatique', an expository
character through whose dialogue with the protagonist the
audience learns the details it needs for comprehension of the
play. The news (III.iii) that Thésée is alive and his return
imminent is a 'péripétie' or sudden change of fortune, and
coming as it does after Phèdre's declaration of love to Hippolyte it constitutes a 'coup de théâtre', a sudden dramatic
surprise. Such description will show that *Phèdre* is a well-made
play by the standards of its day, but the modern reader will
need to know more. We shall look at the structure of the play
by considering a number of its elements, including story,
characters, setting, time, and imagery.

The story of Phèdre

If we summarise the events which constitute the plot of *Phèdre*
and see how these events are arranged through the five acts of
the play (their 'disposition', in rhetorical terms), it is clear
both that there are no slack passages or empty acts, and that
there are elements of symmetry and design which make the
'disposition' pleasing. The main elements in the plot are
distributed among the acts as follows:

Act I – Hippolyte announces his intention of leaving, and
admits his love of Aricie to his confidant. Phèdre admits her
love of Hippolyte to her confidant. Thésée's death is reported
to Phèdre.

19

[Between Acts I and II, Troezen recognizes Hippolyte as king, and Hippolyte requests an interview with Aricie.]

Act II – Aricie admits her love of Hippolyte to her confidant. Hippolyte declares his love to Aricie. Phèdre declares her love to Hippolyte. A rumour that Thésée is still alive is reported to Hippolyte.

Act III – Thésée's arrival is reported to Phèdre, and her confidant plans to save Phèdre's reputation by slandering Hippolyte. Thésée is troubled by the strange behaviour first of Phèdre, and then of Hippolyte.

Act IV – Phèdre's confidant is in the middle of her false story to Thésée as the act opens. Thésée confronts Hippolyte, curses him, and banishes him, disbelieving his protestation of innocence and his claim to be in love with Aricie. Phèdre, on the point of confessing to Thésée, learns both of the curse and of Hippolyte's revelation that he loves Aricie. She is profoundly shaken and murderously jealous.

Act V – Hippolyte and Aricie plan to elope. Thésée, after speaking to Aricie, resolves to seek further enlightenment. He learns of Œnone's suicide and Phèdre's distracted and despairing state. Thésée regrets his curse and hopes it will not be fulfilled by Neptune. Théramène reports the death of Hippolyte. Phèdre, who has taken poison, insists that Thésée hear her clear Hippolyte's name before dying. To appease Hippolyte's spirit, Thésée will adopt Aricie.

Several things are apparent from this summary. First, the significant revelations or developments are well spaced through the play, so that there are no weak or dragging passages. The 'peripeteia' of Thésée's return is centrally placed in the third act. The events of the first two acts having been determined by Thésée's absence and reported death, his return is the catalyst to what happens in the last two acts. Furthermore there is another peripeteia, in Act IV (Phèdre's volte-face when she was on the point of confessing to Thésée), which keeps up the tension at a point where five-act plays sometimes sag.

Patterning is very striking in the opening acts. Hippolyte's reluctant confession to Théramène is followed by Phèdre's even more reluctant confession to Œnone. The scene in which Hippolyte declares his morally innocent love to Aricie is initiated by Hippolyte in order to tell Aricie of the end of her captivity, since the news of Thésée's death makes him ruler in Troezen. It is followed by the corresponding and contrasting scene in which Phèdre declares her morally transgressive love to Hippolyte, in an interview which she initiated as a political dialogue in order to reconcile their interests in the succession to Thésée.

Another element in the pattern is introduced by Hippolyte's opening words, 'Je pars' (I am leaving). This announcement makes an extremely startling opening to the play, and creates an expectation which is constantly denied. In Act III, with Thésée's return, the ostensible motive for Hippolyte's departure has gone; but at last he does go, not voluntarily, seeking his father, but banished by him; not on a heroic quest but to his death. It is as if, although he announces his departure in the first line of the play, he cannot leave until the tragic trap is ready to be sprung. There is a similar patterning in the case of Phèdre. When we first hear of her she is 'Une femme mourante, et qui cherche à mourir' (line 44; a woman who is dying and who seeks to die), but her death, like Hippolyte's departure, is deferred. She cannot die until she has destroyed Hippolyte.

The people of Phèdre

The people of *Phèdre* will be discussed in detail later in this chapter (see 'Protagonists', p. 52 below), but three ways in which their deployment relates to the structure of the play will be mentioned here. First, Phèdre, Thésée, Hippolyte, and Aricie are bound together by tight family connections which not only help to create a sense of intimacy but also form an element in the design. In Act I Thésée is absent and we meet only two members of his family, his son and his wife. At the end of the play both of these are dead and Thésée is seen trying to reconstruct a family by giving Aricie (who is his kinswoman) a place she should have been able to claim as Hippolyte's wife – a place as his daughter:

> Que malgré les complots d'une injuste famille
> Son amante aujourd'hui me tienne lieu de fille!   (V.vi.1653)

(In spite of the plotting of her unrighteous family, let his lover today be as a daughter to me!)

Shrunken and mutilated, the family is reconstituted and the pattern is complete.

The people of *Phèdre* illustrate the structure in another way too. There are thirty scenes in the play (by the conventions prevailing, a new scene begins whenever any character enters or leaves the stage; thus a scene can be very short like V.ii which is only three lines long, as another scene begins when Ismène is dismissed). Although the scenes vary greatly in length, each nevertheless constitutes a unit, and inspection suggests that the number of scenes in which the main characters are present is a reasonable reflection of their importance. Hippolyte, Phèdre, and Thésée are each on stage for twelve scenes, Aricie for only half that number (and Œnone, Phèdre's confidant, for nine). Moreover since Thésée does not appear until after the middle of Act III, he achieves his equal presence by being on stage for all but four out of the remaining sixteen scenes. Again, Hippolyte and Phèdre each have one scene of soliloquy (speaking alone on stage), Thésée has two. Of course these arithmetical considerations are not evident as we read or watch the play, but they bear out a sense of order and balance communicated as the play unfolds, and in the case of Thésée they show how Racine has made sure that in spite of his late entry this character is prominent and weighty in the economy of the play.

Thirdly, the characters stand in relationships of knowledge and ignorance. Hippolyte does not know that Phèdre loves him, so is unwary of her, and deeply horrified by her declaration. Phèdre does not know that Hippolyte loves Aricie, so can briefly delude herself, even after his horror at her confession of love, that she may still win him over; discovery of the truth is an appalling experience for her. All the characters are misled by the false news of Thésée's death, and the actions taken or words spoken, motivated by that false news, are revealed as mistaken or perilous upon his return. Thésée knows of neither Phèdre's love nor Hippolyte's, and is therefore easily deceived by Œnone (in spite of an inner voice which urges him to believe his son innocent). This network of knowledge and ignorance is enhanced in the case of knowledge which is deliberately kept secret. Phèdre has been keeping her love secret even from Œnone. The secret was harmful only to herself as long as she shared it with no-one. Once she has revealed it to Œnone, it becomes possible to reveal it to Hippolyte. Hippolyte tells Théramène of his love for Aricie, then confesses it to Aricie, but continues to conceal it from Thésée until too late – when he does produce it as evidence that he is innocent of the charge of assaulting Phèdre, Thésée thinks it is a poor invention he has just devised. This intricate pattern of knowledge and ignorance, secrecy and deception, is resolved by Phèdre's confession in the last scene. It would not be enough for her to die in expiation of her incestuous, adulterous love and her part in Hippolyte's death – she must also, over Thésée's protests, make the truth known before she dies.

Setting

The setting of *Phèdre* was conceived by Racine as 'a vaulted palace', as we know from the records of the Hôtel de Bourgogne, and from line 854 of the play, but later directors have sometimes preferred to set it outside the palace, or on a portico, where Phèdre can more plausibly come to 'look for daylight' (line 168; also lines 149, 155, 166), and Hippolyte can appear in the opening lines to be on the very point of departure. It might seem that the restricted setting of this play, which follows even more strictly than some other seventeenth-century tragedies the requirement of unity of place, could provide only a fixed and somewhat characterless element in the structure of the play. This is not the case, however. First, whatever stage setting may be provided in performance or imagined in reading, the scene is gradually constructed for us by what characters say about it, and what they say about it changes in the course of the play. In the opening lines Hippolyte refers to Troezen as 'aimable' (pleasant), but a few lines later he describes it as a place he dare not stay in (line 25), attributing his changed attitude first to the presence of Phèdre and then, more truthfully, to that of Aricie. To Phèdre it is the place of exile to which she had had Hippolyte sent from Athens in order to remove him from her sight and try to regain her peace of mind, only to find herself brought to Troezen in her turn, and into a proximity which torments her but which she cannot abandon ('Je ne le puis quitter' (line 763; I cannot leave him)). To Aricie it is the place where, entrusted like Phèdre to Hippolyte's charge, she endures captivity and mourns her dead brothers. To Thésée upon his return it is a place where he had expected to be warmly welcomed after his sinister adventures, but which he finds pervaded with a mysterious horror, which causes his family to shrink from greeting him and rapidly undermines his heroic spirit:

> Je n'ai pour tout accueil que des frémissements:
> Tout fuit, tout se refuse à mes embrassements;
> Et moi-même, éprouvant la terreur que j'inspire,
> Je voudrais être encor dans les prisons d'Epire.   (III.v.975)

(I am greeted only by shudders; everyone flees, everyone refuses my embrace. And as for me, feeling the terror I inspire, I wish myself back in the dungeons of Epirus.)

When Œnone fabricates the story of Hippolyte having assaulted Phèdre, Troezen is represented as the place where a guilty passion, conceived in Athens, has come into the open; ironically, this is true, but true of Phèdre not of Hippolyte, whose passion for Aricie can hardly be seen as guilty even though he feels guilt about it. In Aricie's words, Troezen is a place inhabited by a monster which has survived Thésée's purge:

> Prenez garde, Seigneur: vos invincibles mains
> Ont de monstres sans nombre affranchi les humains,
> Mais tout n'est pas détruit, et vous en laissez vivre
> Un...   (V.iii.1443)

(Beware, my lord: your undefeated hands have freed the human race from countless monsters; but all are not destroyed, and you have left alive *one* . . .)

Finally, to Hippolyte just before he leaves Troezen, it has become 'un lieu funeste et profané / Où la vertu respire un air empoisonné' (line 1359; a deathly, desecrated place, where virtue breathes a poisoned air) – very different from Troezen as evoked by Théramène in the first scene: 'ces paisibles lieux si chers à votre enfance' (line 30; this peaceful place so dear to your childhood).

This evolution of the setting is an important element in the structure of the play, accompanying the movement of events towards disaster. But the immediate stage-scene is not the only element of place. There are other places, just off-stage or further away, which constitute the world of the play. Beginning with the nearest, there are the hidden rooms of the palace, the forest, and the sea.

We know little of the rest of the palace, sensing it only as the place where Phèdre has spent her recent sleepless, fasting days and nights and where she has been dressed and ornamented before emerging (I.iii) to greet the sun for the last time. Just before Thésée's return, the palace setting becomes a threatening force, like a righteous guardian of conjugal values ready to report to Thésée on his dishonoured wife:

> Il me semble déjà que ces murs, que ces voûtes
> Vont prendre la parole, et prêts à m'accuser,
> Attendent mon époux pour le désabuser.   (III.iii.854)

(Already I feel as if these walls and arches will speak, and ready to accuse me they are waiting to disillusion my husband.)

The forest is Hippolyte's domain because he hunts there, and Phèdre longs to be in its shady depths, both to cool her fever and to see Hippolyte. Later she imagines Hippolyte and Aricie together there, in an amorous idyll which has never happened. The forest is both wild and pure, like Hippolyte himself.

The sea is present in our minds not only when Théramène relates the death of Hippolyte which takes place beside it, but before that when we are reminded of Phèdre's origin across the sea in Crete, and even earlier when Théramène describes the travels he has undertaken in his search for Thésée. These lines of Théramène constitute a rapid glimpse of the world beyond Troezen, as well as introducing the theme of the Underworld, and the death of a young man (Icarus):

> Et dans quels lieux, Seigneur, l'allez-vous donc chercher?
> Déjà pour satisfaire à votre juste crainte,
> J'ai couru les deux mers que sépare Corinthe;
> J'ai demandé Thésée aux peuples de ces bords
> Où l'on voit l'Achéron se perdre chez les morts;
> J'ai visité l'Elide, et laissant le Ténare,
> Passé jusqu'à la mer qui vit tomber Icare.   (I.i.8)

(And where, my lord, will you look for him? Already, to satisfy your legitimate fears, I have sailed the two seas either side of Corinth [the Ionian and the Aegean]; I have sought Thésée among the people living on those shores where the River Acheron disappears into the land of the dead [celebrated as one of the rivers of the Underworld, the Acheron flows into Lake Acherusia in Epirus, where Thésée later reveals he has been held captive]. I have been to Elis [plain of the north-west Peloponnese, famous for horse-breeding; perhaps there is a hidden allusion to Hippolyte's name, which in Greek means 'horse-looser' or 'horse-tamer'; it is also the site of a precinct sacred to Hades, lord of the Underworld], and going beyond Taenarum [southern tip of the Peloponnese, site of another supposed entrance to the Underworld], have travelled as far as the sea which saw Icarus fall [the sea is the Aegean, named after Thésée's father; Icarus drowned in it while escaping from Crete and from Phèdre's father].)

Further points in this off-stage geography are the distant home of Hippolyte's Amazon mother and Crete, seat of Phèdre's family, where Thésée as a young man entered the labyrinth to kill the Minotaur, guided by Phèdre's sister.

Beyond this again is the geography, or cosmography, of the supernatural. When Phèdre emerges into sunlight it affects her in a literal, physical way (she is weak and ill, the Greek sun is fierce), but she also regards the sun as her ancestor (lines 169, 1274), and indeed her supernatural ancestors are everywhere: 'Le ciel, tout l'univers est plein de mes aïeux' (line 1276; the sky, the whole universe is full of my ancestors). Below as well as above the earth, Phèdre's family is in command. Death offers no escape, for her father judges the souls of all the dead in the Underworld (line 1280). Topography and mythology are fused here, and this evocation of a world beyond the stage, haunted by the deeds of humans and gods, is one of the ways in which Racine bridges the gap between the beliefs appropriate to the characters in his play, and those of his audience. He does not require us to believe in Minos and the sun-god, but we must understand that Phèdre does.

Time and timelessness

Just as space in *Phèdre* transcends the limits imposed by the unity of place, so time escapes from those imposed by the twenty-four-hour rule. It does this in two opposite but perhaps complementary ways. First, there are many references to time past, and some to projected future time.

References to time past, like references to place, include both close and distant points. In I.iii, Œnone refers to the three days and nights which have passed since Phèdre last ate or slept (the elaborate phrasing not only providing emphasis but suggesting the living, supernatural beings who control the processes of nature):

> Les ombres par trois fois ont obscurci les cieux
> Depuis que le sommeil n'est entré dans vos yeux;
> Et le jour a trois fois chassé la nuit obscure
> Depuis que votre corps languit sans nourriture.   (I.iii.191)

(Darkness has three times darkened the heavens since sleep last entered your eyes; and day has three times chased away dark night while your body has languished without food.)

The next closest point on the time-scale is six months ago; Thésée has been absent for six months, and during that time the other characters have been in Troezen, Aricie and Phèdre placed under Hippolyte's guardianship. Other references are clustered round earlier events in the lives of the protagonists; in particular, Thésée's career as monster-killer and womaniser is evoked by several characters. His victory over the Minotaur in the labyrinth is most strikingly recalled by Phèdre when she re-creates the story, casting herself and Hippolyte in the parts played by her sister Ariane (Ariadne) and Thésée. People's origins or birth are also evoked. Hippolyte's Amazonian mother is cited as a clue to his 'farouche' (shy, untamed) character, and the reference to Phèdre as 'La fille de Minos et de Pasiphaé' suggests both moral judgement (Minos) and sexual waywardness (Pasiphaë). Beyond this there stretches a further past (like the further space extending beyond the immediate off-stage space), which links the protagonists with supernatural ancestors. This past can intrude into the present of the play in Phèdre's sense of herself as having been cursed, like other members of her family, by the goddess of love, and in Thésée's appeal to the sea-god (his putative father, in some versions of the Theseus-myth) to destroy Hippolyte.

Projections of future time can only be misleading or illusory. Hippolyte will not set off from Troezen to look for Thésée. Decisions about how to divide the inheritance of Attica, Troezen, and Crete are pointless, for Thésée is not dead. Phèdre's false vision of an Hippolyte who has repulsed her only because he has never loved before, and may yet prove susceptible, is replaced by an equally distorted vision of an Hippolyte who loves every woman but her. Hippolyte will never marry Aricie – he is killed before he gets to the temple where they were to meet. The subtlest representation of projected time is Phèdre's vision of a 'might-have-been' adventure in the labyrinth of Knossos, narrated in the tenses of possibility and potentiality unrealised – the past conditional and the past subjunctive (lines 649–62). This is a story which can never take place because it has already happened differently.

The complementary method of transcending the unity of time works through a dissolving of the present moment into a sort of timelessness. Shakespeare in *The Tempest* reminds us constantly that (for once) he is observing the unity of time. Racine in *Bajazet* also draws attention to the constraints of time, creating a sense of desperate urgency and frantic activity which must be completed within an unknown time-limit (since the Sultan may return at any time). In *Phèdre* there are only occasional references to the time-span within which the action is taking place, as in Phèdre's words:

Je mourais ce matin digne d'être pleurée;
J'ai suivi tes conseils, je meurs déshonorée.   (III.iii.837)

(I was ready to die this morning, worthy of being mourned; I followed your advice, I die dishonoured.)

At other times we are more aware of the intensity of action
and feeling than of its duration, while certain 'classical' qualities of Racine's language (its restricted vocabulary, abundant
use of abstractions, mythological allusions, and traditional
imagery) enable the text to have a universal quality which does
not weaken its appropriateness to the particular situation
within the play. Phèdre describes falling in love with Hippolyte:

> A peine au fils d'Egée
> Sous les lois de l'hymen je m'étais engagée,
> Mon repos, mon bonheur semblait être affermi,
> Athènes me montra mon superbe ennemi.
> Je le vis, je rougis, je pâlis à sa vue;
> Un trouble s'éleva dans mon âme éperdue;
> Mes yeux ne voyaient plus, je ne pouvais parler,
> Je sentis tout mon corps et transir et brûler.
> Je reconnus Vénus et ses feux redoutables,
> D'un sang qu'elle poursuit tourments inévitables.   (I.iii.269)

(I had only just bound myself to the son of Aegeus [Theseus] under
the laws of marriage, my peace of mind and happiness seemed
assured; Athens showed me my proud foe. I saw him, I blushed, I
went pale at sight of him [or: in his sight]; turmoil arose in my
distraught mind. I could not see, I could not speak. I felt my whole
body grow both cold and hot. I recognised Venus and her dreadful
fires, torments inevitable in blood attacked by her [or: a race pursued
by her].)

This is a narrative of an individual experience set at a precise
moment (shortly after Phèdre's marriage) in a specific place
(Athens). But with its references to fever and chills, blushes
and pallor, as well as to the classical goddess of love, it recalls
a whole European tradition of love-poetry, and seems to
represent an archetypal expression of love at first sight. Hippolyte's account of falling in love with Aricie acquires similar
status by drawing on other elements from the same tradition

such as the lover as slave or captive, love as an arrow which wounds, the loss of selfhood:

> Asservi maintenant sous la commune loi,
> Par quel trouble me vois-je emporté loin de moi?
> Un moment a vaincu mon audace imprudente;
> Cette âme si superbe est enfin dépendante.
> Depuis près de six mois, honteux, désespéré,
> Portant partout le trait dont je suis déchiré,
> Contre vous, contre moi, vainement je m'éprouve   (II.ii.535)

(Enslaved now beneath the universal law [of love], by what turmoil I find myself driven away from myself! One instant conquered my rash boldness; my proud soul is now dependent on another. For almost six months, ashamed and desperate, carrying about with me the arrow which lacerates me, in vain I have pitted my strength against you, against myself)

Imagery

Racine's images are not original but they form a powerful element both in the poetic and emotional effects created by the play and in its structure. Racine uses them to form networks of association through the play, with image-clusters overlapping with each other and also with literal reality. To give a brief example of this last point, the overlap between metaphor and the literal, at lines 991 and 1360 Hippolyte is speaking metaphorically when he uses the words 'poison' and 'empoisonné' (poisoned, poisonous), and so is Phèdre when she uses the word 'empoisonner' (line 1308), but Phèdre then chooses poison as her means of suicide. The development of a set of images throughout the play can be seen by following through the references to light and dark, or monsters, or blood. Examination of one, the most complex, of these will show Racine's technique.

Light and dark can symbolise innocence and evil; thus Hippolyte says 'Le jour n'est pas plus pur que le fond de mon cœur' (line 1112; Day is not purer than my inmost heart) while Phèdre refers to her love, in a phrase which is an oxymoron (contradiction in terms), as 'une flamme si noire' (line 310; so dark a flame). But they also symbolise life and death, thus Œnone refers to Phèdre's fragile life as 'une faible lumière' (line 229; a feeble light) and Phèdre talks about suicide as a flight into 'la nuit infernale' (line 1277; the darkness of the Underworld). Light is associated with the brilliance of the sun, hard for a sick woman to bear, and with the accusing gaze of the sun-god from whom Phèdre claims descent, as well as with the untroubled freedom in which Phèdre imagines Hippolyte and Aricie enjoying their love: 'Tous les jours se levaient clairs et sereins pour eux' (line 1240; Every day dawned clear and fair for them). Darkness is not only evil but, as cool shade, offers concealment from the pitiless sun and is associated with the forest where Phèdre pictures Hippolyte. These images of light and dark (of which there are many more examples) are prominent in the last lines of the play. Thésée after hearing of Hippolyte's death tells Phèdre he wants no 'odieuses lumiéres' (hateful light) cast on what has happened, but will seek concealment and solitude to mourn his son (his words at lines 1608–11 strongly recalling Phèdre's at 1276–7). Phèdre insists on casting that light, in order to clear Hippolyte's name, leaving her hearers, as Thésée says, 'trop éclaircis' (too much enlightened); and as her sight dims with the approach of death she gives final expression to the light/dark imagery:

> Déjà je ne vois plus qu'à travers un nuage
> Et le ciel et l'époux que ma présence outrage;
> Et la mort, à mes yeux dérobant la clarté,
> Rend au jour qu'ils souillaient toute sa pureté.   (V.vii.1641)

(Already I can only dimly see the sky and my husband, outraged by my presence; and death, robbing my eyes of light, restores to the daylight, which they sullied, all its purity.)

Death is commonly associated with darkness; and in the traditional love-poetry to which Racine so often alludes in this play the eyes of a beautiful woman shed light. Both these conventional ideas are reversed here. The 'flamme si noire' (dark flame) of Phèdre's love made her eyes a source of darkness, and death by closing them removes that stain and so becomes paradoxically a source of brightness. This restoration of light is paralleled a moment later, in the closing lines of the play, by Thésée's words promising expiation and appeasement as his own share in the reconstruction of a moral order: although Thésée's speech has the prominent final position, it is Phèdre's words that the reader is more likely to remember, with their extraordinary reworking of the light/dark imagery.

Language

Racine's plays are notoriously difficult to render successfully into English, and *Phèdre* in particular has been described as untranslatable. The difficulties have many causes, but prominent among them are the differences between English and French prosody, and the nature of Racine's vocabulary and diction. There are also difficulties which always attend the translation of poetry (such as the problem of trying to match sound effects), and those which occur in translating into English from any language which, like French, has a choice of formal and intimate forms for the second person singular, a choice which has disappeared from modern English.

In this section, we shall examine an extract from *Phèdre* to show what sort of effects Racine achieves by his use of language, and what sort of knowledge is needed for the reader to notice and enjoy them. Two elements in this knowledge were more widespread among Racine's contemporaries than they are among a modern audience or readership, even a modern French one. These are knowledge of the workings of the alexandrine line which was the normal metre for neo-classical tragedy, and knowledge of classical antiquity.

The alexandrine

The alexandrine is a twelve-syllable line which takes its name from its use in a late twelfth-century epic *Le Roman d'Alexandre*. It was used, although not exclusively, in neo-classical tragedy from the mid sixteenth century on, and in the seventeenth century its use was standard, although this did not exclude the occasional use of other metres for passages which needed to be differentiated from the rest of the text for some reason (such as the choric passages in Racine's biblical tragedies, and the text of a letter in his Turkish play *Bajazet*).

French poetry, unlike most English poetry, works on an exact syllable count. Unlike Latin verse, where syllables are 'quantified' as long or short, any sounded syllable in French counts as having the same metric value, although obviously when the verse is spoken not all syllables will have the same weight or emphasis. So-called 'mute e' (*e atone*) at the end of a word counts as a syllable if it is followed by a consonant or aspirate 'h', except at the end of a line. If it is followed by another vowel or by mute 'h', it is elided with the next word and does not count as a syllable. When a word ends in *e atone* followed by 's' or 'nt', the 'mute' syllable must be counted before a following word in the same line, whether beginning with a vowel or a consonant. In the following lines, the mute 'e's which have the value of a syllable are underlined, those which are elided or dropped are bracketed:

> La mort aux malheureux ne cause point d'effroi;
> Je ne crains que le nom que je laiss[e] après moi.
> Pour mes tristes enfants quel affreux héritag[e]!
> Le sang de Jupiter doit enfler leur courag[e];
> Mais, quelque just[e] orgueil qu'inspir[e] un sang si beau,
> Le crime d'une mèr[e] est un pesant fardeau.   (III.iii.859)

Many actors nowadays do not, in speaking verse, give much syllabic value to these mute 'e's before consonants, although some will allow pauses, or extend the length of other syllables, to make the two halves of the line agree in duration.

Rhymes are classified as 'feminine' (ending in 'e', 'es', or 'ent' not counted in the measure of the line) or 'masculine' (all other endings) and French seventeeth-century verse-drama, like other long poetic forms, is usually in rhyming couplets in which these two forms of rhyme alternate. The conventional nature of the distinction can be seen in the fact that in the following couplet, 'inanimée' and 'pâmée' form a feminine rhyme, whereas if the two participial adjectives referred to Hippolyte rather than Aricie, and were therefore in the masculine form 'inanimé' and 'pâmé', the rhyme would be masculine even though there would be no phonetic difference between this and the feminine rhyme:

> Et froide, gémissante, et presque inanimée,
> Aux pieds de son amant elle tombe pâmée.   (V.vi.1585)

The classical alexandrine normally has a cesura (a metrical pause, coinciding with some degree of syntactical break) after the sixth syllable, thus there is an accent or stress on the sixth syllable and another on the twelfth. Within the six-syllable groups thus formed (hemistichs) there is usually one other stress, dependent on syntax, and the distribution of stresses can vary considerably. In the following three lines from the last scene of *Phèdre*, the grouping of syllables varies from line to line, and the groups are oxytonic, that is to say there will be a slight stress on the last sounded syllable of each group:

```
        2   |    4            ||    3     |   3
    Eh bien! | vous triomphez, || et mon fils | est sans vie.
      1 |      5               ||       6
    Ah! | que j'ai lieu de craindr[e]?  || et qu'un cruel soupçon
      3    |     3            ||   2    |    4
    L'excusant | dans mon cœur, || m'alarm[e] | avec raison!
```
$$\text{(V.vii.1594)}$$

Sometimes the main pause in a line comes elsewhere than at the sixth syllable, as in the second line of the two following:

> Il faut d'un vain amour étouffer la pensée,
> Madame. Rappelez votre vertu passée   (III.iii.825)

A line can also be divided between speakers; here, three speakers are heard in the space of two lines:

ARICIE

Hippolyte aimerait? Par quel bonheur extrême
Aurais-je pu fléchir ...

ISMENE

> Vous l'entendrez lui-même:

Il vient à vous.

HIPPOLYTE

> Madame, avant que de partir
> (II.i–ii.461)

To an ear accustomed to the stronger beat of English verse, the French line may sound rather monotonous at first; but once the basic pattern is grasped, the listener begins to be aware of the varied rhythms within the constant metre, as well as of other sound-patterns such as, in the lines of Thésée quoted above (lines 1594–6), those created by the repetition of the

sounds of 'triomphez' in 'et mon fils', or by the repetition of
the 'cr' sound in the next line.

Classical antiquity

Racine, like other neo-classical playwrights, assumed that a
good proportion of his audience and readership would be
acquainted with the best-known myths, legends, and historical episodes of classical antiquity, transmitted by the
ancient authors and their Renaissance imitators. In *Phèdre*,
as in his other plays on subjects used by Greek dramatists, *La
Thébaïde*, *Andromaque*, and *Iphigénie*, he plays off the known
against the unknown, making changes to the story-material
which would slightly unbalance a first-time spectator or
reader familiar with earlier treatments of the subject. But it is
not so much the main story that the reader needs to know
(since the play will reveal this), as a whole range of allusions
and associations, some of them drawn from the general
mythical background (Neptune's associations with earth-
quakes, bulls, and the taming of horses; the fact that the
goddess who presides over Hippolyte's favourite sport of
hunting is also associated with chastity) and some from the
specific network of the Theseus-myth and the stories associated with Crete (Theseus' reputation as a killer of monsters,
and his abandonment of Phaedra's sister Ariadne on Naxos;
Minos king of Crete and his wife Pasiphaë, who fell in love
with a bull; the Minotaur, half-man and half-bull, born from
that unnatural liaison; the labyrinth, designed and built by
Daedalus to conceal the Minotaur; the flight and fall of
Daedalus' son Icarus while trying to escape from Crete with
his father after the construction of the labyrinth, which
Minos wished to keep secret).

An examination of some ninety lines from the fourth act
of *Phèdre* will illustrate all these points. In IV.iv, Phèdre
learns from Thésée (who does not himself believe it) that
Hippolyte is in love with Aricie. After twenty-one lines of
anguished soliloquy, Phèdre is joined (IV.vi) by her confidant,
Œnone:

PHEDRE

Chère Œnone, sais-tu ce que je viens d'apprendre?

ŒNONE

Non; mais je viens tremblante, à ne vous point mentir.   1215
J'ai pâli du dessein qui vous a fait sortir;
J'ai craint une fureur à vous-même fatale.

PHEDRE

Œnone, qui l'eût cru? j'avais une rivale!

ŒNONE

Comment?

PHEDRE

Hippolyte aime, et je n'en puis douter.
Ce farouche ennemi qu'on ne pouvait dompter,   1220
Qu'offensait le respect, qu'importunait la plainte,
Ce tigre, que jamais je n'abordai sans crainte,
Soumis, apprivoisé, reconnaît un vainqueur:
Aricie a trouvé le chemin de son cœur.

ŒNONE

Aricie?

PHEDRE

Ah! douleur non encore éprouvée!   1225
A quel nouveau tourment je me suis réservée!
Tout ce que j'ai souffert, mes craintes, mes transports,
La fureur de mes feux, l'horreur de mes remords,
Et d'un cruel refus l'insupportable injure,
N'était qu'un faible essai des tourments que j'endure.   1230
Ils s'aiment! Par quel charme ont-ils trompé mes yeux?
Comment se sont-ils vus? depuis quand? dans quels lieux?
Tu le savais. Pourquoi me laissais-tu séduire?
De leur furtive ardeur ne pouvais-tu m'instruire?
Les a-t-on vus souvent se parler, se chercher?   1235
Dans le fond des forêts allaient-ils se cacher?
Hélas! ils se voyaient avec pleine licence.
Le ciel de leurs soupirs approuvait l'innocence;
Ils suivaient sans remords leur penchant amoureux;
Tous les jours se levaient clairs et sereins pour eux.   1240
Et moi, triste rebut de la nature entière,
Je me cachais au jour, je fuyais la lumière.
La mort est le seul dieu que j'osais implorer.
J'attendais le moment où j'allais expirer;
Me nourrissant de fiel, de larmes abreuvée,   1245
Encor dans mon malheur de trop près observée,
Je n'osais dans mes pleurs me noyer à loisir.

Je goûtais en tremblant ce funeste plaisir,
Et, sous un front serein déguisant mes alarmes,
Il fallait bien souvent me priver de mes larmes.   1250

                    ŒNONE
Quel fruit recevront-ils de leurs vaines amours?
Ils ne se verront plus.

                    PHEDRE
              Ils s'aimeront toujours!
Au moment que je parle, ah! mortelle pensée!
Ils bravent la fureur d'une amante insensée.
Malgré ce même exil qui va les écarter,   1255
Ils font mille serments de ne se point quitter.
Non, je ne puis souffrir un bonheur qui m'outrage,
Œnone; prends pitié de ma jalouse rage;
Il faut perdre Aricie, il faut de mon époux
Contre un sang odieux réveiller le courroux.   1260
Qu'il ne se borne pas à des peines légères:
Le crime de la sœur passe celui des frères.
Dans mes jaloux transports je le veux implorer.
Que fais-je? Où ma raison va-t-elle s'égarer?
Moi jalouse! Et Thésée est celui que j'implore!   1265
Mon époux est vivant, et moi je brûle encore!
Pour qui? Quel est le cœur où prétendent mes vœux?
Chaque mot sur mon front fait dresser mes cheveux.
Mes crimes désormais ont comblé la mesure.
Je respire à la fois l'inceste et l'imposture;   1270
Mes homicides mains, promptes à me venger,
Dans le sang innocent brûlent de se plonger.
Misérable! et je vis? et je soutiens la vue
De ce sacré soleil dont je suis descendue?
J'ai pour aïeul le père et le maître des dieux;   1275
Le ciel, tout l'univers est plein de mes aïeux;
Où me cacher? Fuyons dans la nuit infernale.
Mais que dis-je? Mon père y tient l'urne fatale;
Le sort, dit-on, l'a mise en ses sévères mains:
Minos juge aux enfers tous les pâles humains.   1280
Ah! combien frémira son ombre épouvantée,
Lorsqu'il verra sa fille à ses yeux présentée,
Contrainte d'avouer tant de forfaits divers,
Et des crimes peut-être inconnus aux enfers!
Que diras-tu, mon père, à ce spectacle horrible?   1285
Je crois voir de ta main tomber l'urne terrible,
Je crois te voir, cherchant un supplice nouveau,
Toi-même, de ton sang devenir le bourreau.

Pardonne! Un dieu cruel a perdu ta famille:
Reconnais sa vengeance aux fureurs de ta fille.   1290
Hélas! du crime affreux dont la honte me suit,
Jamais mon triste cœur n'a recueilli le fruit;
Jusqu'au dernier soupir de malheurs poursuivie,
Je rends dans les tourments une pénible vie.

ŒNONE

Hé! repoussez, Madame, une injuste terreur!   1295
Regardez d'un autre œil une excusable erreur.
Vous aimez. On ne peut vaincre sa destinée.
Par un charme fatal vous fûtes entraînée.
Est-ce donc un prodige inouï parmi nous?
L'amour n'a-t-il encor triomphé que de vous?   1300
La faiblesse aux humains n'est que trop naturelle;
Mortelle, subissez le sort d'une mortelle.
Vous vous plaignez d'un joug imposé dès longtemps:
Les dieux mêmes, les dieux de l'Olympe habitants,
Qui d'un bruit si terrible épouvantent les crimes,   1305
Ont brûlé quelquefois de feux illégitimes.

(Ph. – Dear Œnone, do you know what I have just learned?
Œ. – No, but to tell you the truth I come trembling.   [1215]
I blanched at your intention when you left the palace;
I feared a madness which would be fatal to you.
Ph.– Œnone, who would have thought it? I had a rival.
Œ. – What?
Ph. –   Hippolyte is in love, and I must believe it.
That fierce enemy whom no one could tame,   [1220]
offended by respect, irritated by lamentation,
that tiger, whom I never addressed without fear,
now, submissive and tamed, acknowledges a conqueror:
Aricie has found the way to his heart.
Œ. – Aricie?
Ph. –   Oh! pain never felt before!   [1225]
For what new torture have I kept myself alive!
All I have suffered, my fears, my violent emotions,
the fury of my passion, the horror of my remorse,
and the intolerable insult of a cruel rejection,
all this was but a weak foretaste of the torture I am enduring. [1230]
They love one another! By what magic have they deceived my eyes?
How have they seen each other? since when? where?
You knew. Why did you let me go astray?
Could you not tell me of their furtive passion?
Have they often been seen talking to one another, looking for one
    another?   [1235]

Did they go off to hide in the depths of the forests?
Alas! they saw each other in complete freedom.
Heaven approved the innocence of their sighs;
they followed the instinct of their love without remorse;
every day rose bright and serene for them.   [1240]
And I, lowest and most wretched creature in the whole of nature,
I hid from day, I fled the light.
Death is the only god to whom I dared pray.
I waited for the moment of my death;
nourished with bile, feeding on tears,   [1245]
and watched too closely in my misery,
I dared not even weep my fill.
I trembled as I tasted that gloomy pleasure,
and hiding my fears behind a serene brow,
I often had to do without my tears.   [1250]
Œ. – What profit will they have from their futile love?
They will never see each other again.
Ph. –   They will love each other for ever!
Now as I speak, oh, thought that kills!
They are defying the fury of a maddened lover.
In spite of that very exile which will separate them,   [1255]
they are swearing a thousand oaths never to part.
No, I cannot endure a happiness which outrages me,
Œnone; take pity on my jealous rage;
Aricie must be destroyed, my husband's anger
against a hateful family must be rekindled.   [1260]
Let him not settle for mild punishment:
the sister's crime exceeds her brothers'.
In my jealous frenzy I will implore him.
What am I doing? Where is my reason straying?
I, jealous! And Thésée to be the one I appeal to!   [1265]
My husband is alive, and I am still in love!
With whom? Whose is the heart my desires are set on?
Every word makes my hair stand on end.
My crimes now have gone beyond all bounds.
Now I am plunged in both incest and deceit;   [1270]
my murderous hands, eager to avenge me,
long to bathe in innocent blood.
Wretch that I am! and I still live? still meet the eye
of that sacred sun from which I am descended?
My ancestor is the father and ruler of the gods;   [1275]
heaven, the whole universe, is full of my forebears;
where can I hide? Let's flee into the night of hell.
But what am I saying? My father is there, holding the urn of fate.
Destiny, they say, has placed it in his strict hands:
Minos judges all pale humans in the Underworld.   [1280]

Oh, how his shade, aghast, will tremble,
when he sees his daughter stand before him,
forced to confess so many varied crimes,
and crimes perhaps that are unknown in hell!
What will you say, father, to this dreadful sight?   [1285]
I think I see the terrible urn drop from your hand,
I think I see you, looking for a new punishment,
become the torturer of your own kin.
Forgive! A cruel god has ruined your family:
recognize the god's vengeance in the madness of your
    daughter.   [1290]
Alas! from the frightful crime whose shame dogs me,
my wretched heart has never gathered any fruit.
Pursued by misfortunes to my last breath,
I give up in torment a painful life.
Œ. – Ah, cast off, my lady, an unfounded fear!   [1295]
Look upon a pardonable error with a different eye.
You are in love. One cannot overcome one's destiny.
You were carried away by a fated spell.
Is this a miracle that has never happened to any of us before?
Has love never triumphed over anyone but you?   [1300]
This weakness is only too natural in humans;
a mortal woman, you must suffer the fate of a mortal woman.
You complain of a yoke imposed long ago:
The gods themselves, the gods dwelling on Olympus,
who threaten crimes with such dire warnings,   [1305]
have sometimes burned with illicit love.)

The line-by-line translation offered here is intended only to aid
comprehension, not to render the qualities of the French.
Even this modest enterprise is difficult, and its results unsatis-
factory, for reasons which themselves throw some light on
Racine's use of language, and will be mentioned in the discussion of Racine's diction.

Diction

Racine's vocabulary, like that of all French seventeenth-
century classical tragedians, is restricted both by the constraints of prosody and by the conventions governing tragic
language, which aimed at a 'noble' and often euphemistic
tone, excluding anything humdrum or vulgar, and almost
eliminating the concrete. Euphemism may be seen in lines

1291–2, where Phèdre is alluding to the fact that she has not made love to Hippolyte, by an unexciting metaphor of sexual pleasure as fruit to be plucked.

One way of coping with the limitations thus imposed on the size of the poet's vocabulary is to exploit ambiguity, and there are several examples of this in the passage quoted. Sometimes it is merely a question of using a word with various meanings or connotations (and such words are hard to translate because there is most unlikely to be another word in the target language with the same array of associations). Such a word is *farouche*, used of Hippolyte in line 1220. The word comes from Low Latin *forasticus*, meaning outsider, stranger, or foreigner (appropriate for Hippolyte who is 'fils de l'Amazone', the Amazon woman's son), and combines the following meanings: shy, timid, fleeing when approached; fierce, savage, wild; inflexible, unflinching. Into two syllables of the line Racine has therefore packed a richly suggestive characterisation of Hippolyte, contrasting with the last two lines of Phèdre's speech which refer to the taming of this wild creature. A similar form of ambiguity, which touches central themes of the play, is that of the word *ciel* which means both sky (for which it is the everyday word) and heaven (in English poetic diction 'heaven' can mean sky, but 'sky' cannot as a rule mean heaven). When Phèdre says of Hippolyte and Aricie 'Le ciel de leurs soupirs approuva l'innocence' (line 1238), the context sustains both meanings of *ciel*. Nearby phrases such as 'avec pleine licence' (line 1237) and 'sans remords' (line 1239), as well as 'approuvait l'innocence' in line 1238 itself, all support the idea of *ciel* as heaven, the home of moral authority. The contrast between the murky 'fond des forêts', the forest depths where the lovers might have hidden, and their supposed freedom to see each other openly, in daylight, allows us also to read 'ciel' as sky, although a semi-personified sky. This aspect of 'ciel' helps to create the force of line 1240, where again the two levels of meaning co-exist; in Phèdre's imagination, the sun shone for these lovers, *and* their days were carefree because untroubled by guilt.

Another kind of ambiguity arises earlier in this speech when

Phèdre demands of Œnone 'Pourquoi me laissais-tu séduire?'
We have translated this by 'Why did you let me go astray?',
since this English phrase can be used for both literal and moral
wanderings, but the French is more subtle. The surface
meaning is 'Why did you let me be misinformed?', but stronger
meanings of *séduire* (charm, seduce) are lurking in the line as
well, so that Phèdre is irrationally blaming Œnone for having
'let' her be charmed or seduced (and 'led astray' from virtue)
by Hippolyte. There is also ambiguity of tone, which is less of
a problem for the translator as a rule. Thus in the last four
lines of Phèdre's second long speech here (1291–4), Phèdre
seems to be justifying herself, pleading that at least, in spite of
her shameful desire, she has not committed incest and adultery. But the introduction of this plea by the word 'Hélas'
(alas), the ambivalence of 'triste' (deplorable or unhappy), and
the content of the final two lines, point to another interpretation of her words, which co-exists with the mitigating plea; in
this second interpretation, the tone is one of regret that she did
not even derive any pleasure from her love, and this failure to
gratify desire is one of the 'malheurs' and 'tourments' which
beset her now.

One characteristic of Racine's language confronting the
translator is his variety of register. This variety is particularly
clever given the requirement of 'noble' diction, and the constraints of rhyme, and it is probably one of the reasons why
Racinian characters seem less stiff than those of most of his
contemporaries writing for the theatre. Racine's language is
rhetorical, inevitably so since his very form (rhyming couplets)
is stylised and artificial, and there is no shortage of rhetorical
schemes and tropes in his verse. Often, to accommodate rhyme
or for emphasis, the word order is different from that of prose,
as in lines 1229, 1234, 1236, 1238, 1245, 1246, 1247, 1249, and
many others. Yet every now and then, on every page of
Racine, come phrases or whole lines which have the simplicity
of everyday prose. Œnone responds to Phèdre's
announcement that she has a rival by a simple 'Comment?'
(line 1219), and Phèdre's continuation of the line is scarcely
more elaborate. A similarly direct and plain note is heard at

lines 1235, 1244, 1262, and elsewhere. Particularly pleasing are
the moments when this direct and simple language co-exists
with strong rhetorical patterning, as happens in this extract at
line 1252. The line is divided symmetrically between the two
speakers, and each hemistich is entirely free of rhetorical
artifice. Together, however, they have a very conspicuous
rhetorical pattern, combining similarity (two third person
plural reflexive verbs in the future tense) and difference
(negative/positive). The similarity reflects the fact that Œnone
and Phèdre are talking about the same thing – what the future
holds for Hippolyte and Aricie; the difference contrasts
Œnone's factual viewpoint with Phèdre's intuitive knowledge.
Reciprocal love is deeply enviable to the rejected lover even if
it is doomed.

Irony

Another of the ways in which Racine extends his linguistic
resources is through irony. We have already pointed out the
ironic contrast between the 'farouche' Hippolyte loved and
feared by Phèdre and the lover of Aricie, 'soumis, apprivoisé'
(submissive and tamed). A more tragic instance of irony (and
closer to the ancient notion of 'tragic irony' where one character lacks the knowledge possessed by another character and
the audience) occurs in Phèdre's evocation of the innocent,
idyllic love she imagines Hippolyte and Aricie enjoying:

> Dans le fond des forêts allaient-ils se cacher?
> Hélas! ils se voyaient avec pleine licence.
> Le ciel de leurs soupirs approuvait l'innocence;
> Ils suivaient sans remords leur penchant amoureux;
> Tous les jours se levaient clairs et sereins pour eux.

Here, the audience is better informed than either of the characters on stage. Œnone appeared surprised when Phèdre told
her that Hippolyte was in love ('Comment?' 'Aricie?'), so
Phèdre's accusation 'Tu le savais' (You knew) was false.
Equally false, we know, is Phèdre's vision of the two lovers
innocently enjoying an acknowledged and legitimate love.

dehis ⌐
5 /

Everything in this picture is inaccurate. At the beginning of
the play, Hippolyte is so distressed by finding himself in love
with Aricie that he wants to leave Troezen; he feels ashamed of
this love not only because Aricie belongs to a proscribed
family, his father's defeated enemies, but also because he is
disturbed to find himself apparently able to imitate his father
only by falling in love, not by heroism and slaying monsters.
Furthermore, we know that Hippolyte and Aricie have only
just admitted their love to each other, and rather one-sidedly
at that, for after Hippolyte's lengthy speech (II.ii.524–60)
setting out his feelings for Aricie, Théramène interrupts to say
that Phèdre is looking for Hippolyte, and Aricie has time only
for an indirect and understated declaration:

> J'accepte tous les dons que vous me voulez faire;
> Mais cet empire enfin si grand, si glorieux,
> N'est pas de vos présents le plus cher à mes yeux.   (II.iii.574)

(I accept all the gifts you wish to make to me: but indeed this great
and glorious empire is not the dearest of your presents in my eyes.)

We know, then, that Phèdre's vision of Hippolyte and Aricie
enjoying each other's company 'avec pleine licence', and under
a clear, approving sky, has been created by her jealous imagination, which envies Hippolyte and Aricie not only the reci-
procity of their love but also its innocence. The error is ironic;
and it is tragically so, for it prevents Phèdre from telling
Thésée the truth and so helps to kill Hippolyte.

Rhythm

Accounts of the effect of rhythm are bound to be personal and
impressionistic, but even a glance at the printed text will
demonstrate that Racine uses a variety of rhythms within the
alexandrine, for in this extract three lines contain a change of
speaker (two of them occurring before the sixth syllable) and
twenty-three others have some mark of punctuation after the
first, second, third, or fourth syllable. Such punctuation indicates a break elsewhere than after the sixth syllable, or in
addition to the regular cesura there. This varies the march of

the six-syllable hemistichs without destroying regularity (the fundamental pattern of rhymed alexandrine couplets is never flawed).

The device of an early break can throw into prominence either the first syllable group or the rest of the line. In line 1234, the phrase 'Tu le savais' (You knew), occupying four syllables, is a short affirmative statement amidst a welter of questions. It is thus distinguished grammatically (indicative, not interrogative, mood) and typographically (no question mark) but also it is rhythmically isolated, which increases the vehemence of the mistaken accusation which it conveys. In line 1237, in contrast, the opening 'Hélas' adds feeling rather than meaning, but the early pause in the line allows the more significant words which follow to be spoken as one long phrase; the vision of Hipppolyte's and Aricie's supposed freedom ('licence') is appropriately expressed by this expansiveness which overflows the six-syllable unit.

Distress or confusion can be communicated through a rapid succession of lines with differently placed breaks. At line 1264, Phèdre's jealous fury is succeeded by a horrified realisation of her own irrationality. She is like someone waking in confusion from a dream, and three of the next four lines suggest this confusion with breaks after the second or third syllable.

Use or absence of *e atone* also affects rhythmic texture. A line in which all syllables have full metrical value has a certain weightiness, which can seem either sumptuous or somewhat oppressive. Lines 1238–40 are of this kind, and this contributes to the richness of the pleasures imagined by Phèdre. In lines 1242–4 there are three such lines in succession (and others at lines 1246–7, 1249–50), and here the lack of 'ventilation' by *e atone* reinforces the calm but bitter hopelessness with which Phèdre recalls what she has been suffering. The presence of *e atone* at a place where it is not elided immediately creates a more interesting rhythm, and also tends to make the preceding syllable seem more important, as with 'crime' and 'passe' in line 1262 and 'pâles' in line 1280. A subtle effect is achieved with the help of *e atone* in line 1302, where its presence at the end of the first use of 'mortelle' isolates the word slightly. This makes the meaning of the line easier to grasp, as well as making the word conspicuous so that its repetition at the end of the line is more marked (this line will be discussed again in connection with the characterisation of Œnone).

Although it is not conspicuous in this extract, one further rhythmic device should be mentioned because elsewhere in the play Racine makes what is probably his most famous use of it. It is the device of enjambment (or 'rejet' in French) whereby a syntactic unit runs over the end of a metrical unit (line or hemistich). Mild examples of this occur in the extract, for example the long delay in lines 1220–3 between subject ('Ce farouche ennemi') and verb ('reconnaît'), which builds up tension by delaying the speaking of Aricie's name. Another common type involves the 'rejet' of a name or title. It occurs in 1258, with Œnone's name, but is less striking here than when Phèdre uses it five times with titles ('Seigneur' and 'Prince') in the scene of her declaration to Hippolyte (lines 585, 597, 624, 630, 666), the effect changing in the course of the scene from a simple emphasising of formality to a futile attempt to reclaim lost ground and regain control over herself and the interview. But the boldest and most celebrated instance in the play is the 'rejet' of the normally insignificant word 'Un' (one) from line 1445 to line 1446 (quoted in 'Structure', p. 24 above), where Aricie leaves unsaid what she has promised Hippolyte not to mention, yet calls Phèdre a monster and succeeds in troubling Thésée and provoking him (too late) into self-interrogation and a quest for enlightenment. There is a kind of wit in such flourishes of metrical skill, which seem to tease the reader or spectator with the possibility of the collapse of form before restoring order and the security of the line.

Rhyme

Rhyme in Racine is usually fairly unobtrusive, but does often serve to give emphasis, not only to the individual word placed at the rhyme, but to relationships between rhyme-words. Thus 'innocence' (line 1238) completes and explains the idea of 'licence' with which it rhymes. The separation of Hippolyte and Aricie is expressed by 'écarter' (line 1255) and contrasted with their vows 'de ne se point quitter' (not to leave one another). The 'courroux' (anger) in line 1260 is that of the 'époux' (husband) in the previous line. Sometimes the effect of the rhyme is enhanced by assonance in nearby syllables, as at lines 1251–2 where the repetition of the vowel sound of 'vaines' in 'aimeront' strengthens the force of 'Ils s'aimeront toujours' (They will love each other for ever) as an answer to Œnone's contemptuous 'vaines amours' (futile love). Sometimes a group of rhymes sound so alike that a unit is created within the longer unit of the speech. Thus the last six lines of Phèdre's second speech are built on three rhymes using the sounds [i] and [ɥi] (famille/fille; suit/fruit; poursuivie/vie). The relationship between these rhymes is reinforced by the alliteration in 'f' of 'famille', 'fille', and 'fruit', and the echo of the [ɥi] sound from 'suit' and 'fruit' in 'poursuivie'. Phèdre has been addressing her father Minos since line 1285, but these last six lines are set apart from the rest as a sort of prayer of penitence, although also a meditation, and, as suggested earlier, an expression of frustration and amoral regret. The identity of this six-line passage within the long speech is marked by the similarity of the three rhymes used.

Imagery

The imagery of light and dark in this scene has already been mentioned in 'Structure', (p. 30 above); it is the most prominent element in the imagery of this passage, but not the only one. The hunting image (which merges into the light/dark imagery through the contrast between bright sunshine outside the forest and cool shade within it) is present in Phèdre's words from the moment she uses the word 'farouche' about Hippolyte, a word with strong wild-beast associations (see 'Diction', p. 41 above). This idea is then reinforced by the word 'dompter' (tame) and made more precise with the use of 'tigre', an animal which is hunted (although not in Greece – but then Hippolyte is half-foreign). The idea of hunting has already been alluded to by Phèdre (line 306) and by Hippolyte (lines 540, 543), and Phèdre now reminds us of this again when she describes herself as in flight like a hunted animal ('Je fuyais la lumière' – I fled the light, line 1242), as though her ancestor the sun, as well as the vindictive goddess of love Venus, is a hunter in pursuit of her. There are also several more or less conventional metaphors for love in this passage. It is a fire (lines 1228, 1266, 1306), its enjoyment is a fruit (lines 1251, 1292), it is associated with magic ('charme', lines 1231, 1298), and with the supernatural (line 1289); and to win someone's love is to defeat them in a battle (line 1223), while to love involuntarily is to have lost a battle (line 1300). None of these metaphors is at all fully developed, so that they nudge at our imagination rather than taking it over completely. But they are all used several times during the play, so that they contribute unobtrusively to its texture and to the close relationship of its parts.

Mythology

This extract illustrates well Racine's use of mythology, at once powerful and tactful. The most striking mythological allusion in this passage, more developed than the references to Phèdre's descent from the sun and Zeus/Jupiter ('le père et le maître des dieux') and to Venus' vindictive pursuit of her (lines 1289–90), is the image (line 1278 to end of speech) of Phèdre's father Minos as judge in the Underworld. This element of the figure of Minos is less well known than his activities on Crete, and Racine handles it tactfully, providing (in line 1280) the information necessary for any reader or spectator who does not know the story of Minos' Underworld career or has forgotten it.

To some extent, Racine allows us to be sceptical or agnostic about the gods of his Greek world. That part of the Theseus-legend which recounts his journey as a living man to the Underworld to try to abduct its queen is alluded to only as the most widespread of the incredible rumours ('incroyables discours', line 380) circulating about his death. Minos 'is said' to have been appointed judge of the Underworld ('dit-on', line

1279). When Phèdre speaks of 'Vénus' this could at times be understood as a metaphor for passionate love ('C'est Vénus tout entiére', line 306). There is no getting away from the idea that a beast comes out of the sea and causes Hippolyte's death, but the possibility that a god urged the bolting horses on is only a rumour, which does not require our assent:

> On dit qu'on a vu même, en ce désordre affreux,
> Un dieu qui d'aiguillons pressait leur flanc poudreux.
>
> (V.vi.1539)

(It is said that some even saw amid this awful chaos a god, goading the horses' dusty flanks.)

Even the bolting of the horses is prepared for by earlier references to Hippolyte's recent neglect of them (lines 550–2). This is not to say that the supernatural dimension in *Phèdre* is unimportant, but that it is presented with a sort of courtesy towards the spectator's scepticism. It must however affect our reactions to the characters of the drama. If the swoops into very simple language, discussed above, reinforce our sense of shared humanity, the mention of divine ancestry counters this by a distancing effect. These people are not like us after all, they belong to the world of myth and to a very distant past. Minos' mother was Europa, whose name our continent bears (and when Zeus abducted her in one of his amorous adventures he appeared in the form of a bull from the sea ...). Phèdre fears the sun not only because she is a sick and fevered woman longing for cool shade, but because it is her accusing maternal grandfather.

closeness/distance

Characterisation

Noting the mythological dimension brings us finally to the question of characterisation. This scene is a dialogue between a principal character and her confidant. Œnone is more developed, more interesting, and perhaps more sinister than most confidants, and is unusual in committing suicide before her mistress, but she still displays several characteristics of the type. She speaks much less than her principal. She is devoted to Phèdre and tries to reassure and comfort her. She is matter-of-fact, although this does not necessarily give her clearer perception than Phèdre (see discussion of lines 1251–2 under 'Diction', above). Œnone is the successor to unnamed characters in Euripides and Seneca who are merely referred to as 'Nurse', and nurses in tragedy are particularly given to making sentensious utterances, lines with a generalising or even proverbial ring to them. Œnone does this in her only substantial speech in this scene. Her first sentensious utterance does not fill the line (1297), the first quarter of the line being a reference to Phèdre. This interweaving of the particular and the general continues, with three lines about Phèdre (1298–1300) being followed by the sentensious line 1301. Line 1302 (mentioned above under 'Rhythm' for its use of *e atone*) is extremely clever. It sounds very rhetorical, with its use of 'mortelle' as first and last word. It elegantly links the particular and the general: the first use of 'mortelle' refers to Phèdre, the second to any mortal woman, and the emphasis on 'mortelle' forms a pleasing contrast with 'Les dieux mêmes, les dieux' who occupy the last three lines of the speech.

To discuss whether this speech is lifelike is beside the point. It is 'typelike', the right sort of speech for a tragic nurse, but at the same time individualised by touches such as the rather casuistic argument which reduces Phèdre's adulterous and incestuous passion to 'une excusable erreur' – this recalls Œnone's earlier assertion that if Thésée was dead, then Phèdre's love became 'une flamme ordinaire' (line 350), overlooking the fact that removing the adulterous element would not remove the incestuous one. The phrase 'habitants de l'Olympe' may seem stilted. Phèdre does not need to be reminded of where the gods live, and the audience does not care. But this is a phrase rendering the Greek word *Olumpios*, dwelling on Olympus, used by Homer and by Greek dramatic poets as an epithet for the gods above, and particularly for Phèdre's ancestor 'le père et le maître des dieux', Zeus himself, whose habit of burning with illicit fires was conspicuous, and indeed the origin of Phèdre's paternal ancestry. It is therefore a further tiny element in creating that distance mentioned above in discussion of mythology, while for the spectator or reader able to pick it up there is an echo here of Greek poetry which will be recognized and give pleasure. Since it is neither enigmatic nor obtrusive, it will not disturb those who do not pick up the allusion.

Phèdre has reached the limit of her endurance in this scene, and her reason is shaken, as she herself comments (line 1264). The pain of frustrated sexual passion, already exacerbated by Hippolyte's reaction to her confession, has now been horribly intensified by jealousy. In IV.v, the short scene just before this one when Phèdre is alone on stage, having just received the news of Hippolyte's love for Aricie, we hear a sort of paranoid distortion enter her view of Hippolyte, as she meditates the possibility that instead of being unsusceptible to women (as she had supposed, finding in this some comfort for his reaction to her) he is in fact ready to love all the women in the world except her (line 1212). Phèdre's speeches in the extract we are examining contain equally deluded elements. There is first the erroneous vision of Hippolyte and Aricie enjoying the pleasures of love in freedom and innocence (lines 1237–40), already commented on. Then there is the wording 'Il faut perdre Aricie' (line 1259; Aricie must be destroyed), using the language of necessity or obligation ('Il faut') to propose the murder of an innocent person. Going further into absurdity or insanity, Phèdre announces her intention of seeking Thésée's help in bringing this about (lines 1259–63). Later in the speech, another marker of an extremely troubled mind is the language of lines 1271–2. Here Phèdre's would-be murderous hands seem to be independently alive, and to experience a desire to kill which is comparable in intensity to Phèdre's desire for Hippolyte, since the verb used of them, 'brûlent', is also used by Phèdre when she is on the brink of confessing her love to Hippolyte: 'Oui, Prince, je languis, je brûle pour Thésée' (line 634; Yes, Prince, I pine, I burn for love of Thésée). Lastly there is Phèdre's direct address to her father and the imagined scene of herself appearing before him, which moves into what could be interpreted as a hallucination, introduced by the repeated phrase 'Je crois voir' (I think I see, lines 1286 and 1287). But the mental disorder which such delusions indicate is balanced by lucidity, a lucidity which operates on two levels, both of them very typical of Racine's theatre. First, Phèdre is represented as able intermittently to perceive her own bizarre state of mind and to comment on it in rational horror, as she does at line 1264. Secondly, there is order and clarity in the representation of even the most disturbed aspects of Phèdre's state of mind. Linguistically there is no suggestion of loss of control or incoherence. Plainly it is not realistic for a woman in a state of jealous rage to be so articulate. But this fluency, although it is far removed from simple realism, is yet what we might call truthful. It enables us to have a clear idea of the various forces active in the character, precisely because those forces are manifested in a very stylised way, whereas if Phèdre were here represented realistically she might weep, moan, scream, or be silent, and we should have to guess at what was going through her mind.

This stylisation is an important aspect of Racine's technique, and means that although his plays have generally been regarded as focusing on the detailed analysis of the states of mind and feeling of characters, their reaction to pressure and crisis, their self-absorption, their pride, their cruelty, and so on, these characters can also be seen in quite a different and more abstract way, not as 'living' human beings (although of course to see the play, or imagine it in performance while reading it, creates a sort of presumption of 'life'), but as something more like essences or idealised representations of pure and absolute states of feeling, or as elements in a network of relationships of forces. Readers can make their own choice among these ways of reading Racine, or indeed hold several in mind at once.

Protagonists

The protagonists in Racine's *Phèdre* engage in little physical action in an ordinary sense; their action is primarily verbal. Of the handful of stage directions to the play, only one describes a straightforward physical act: Phèdre, feeling weak, sits down

(line 157). Attention has been drawn, however, to the 'implicit 6
stage directions' contained in the words of the protagonists
and denoting physical action. A notable example is to be
found in Phèdre's confession of love to Hippolyte (lines
704–11), which ends in a scuffle. The passage is of special
interest in that it evokes a violent physical action in which
Phèdre attempts to kill herself with a stage-property, namely
Hippolyte's sword. Other more common physical movements
are implied: Œnone physically supporting her mistress (line
713), Thésée holding out his arms to embrace his wife (line
914). Emotions, however, are more fundamental to the action
of the play, although they too may manifest themselves
through the evocation of physical movement and changes of
expression. An instructive example is furnished by Phèdre's
words at the beginning of II.v: 'Le voici. Vers mon cœur tout
mon sang se retire' (line 581; He is here. All my blood drains
into my heart). The literal reference is to a physiological
experience, and there is a suggestion of a visual change, the
blood having drained from the face, but the dramatic meaning
is emotional, helped, obviously enough, by the emotional
connotation of the 'heart'. These particular words of Phèdre
function, however, rather as a comment or an aside than as
verbal action, which has been defined as 'a verbal exchange of
a persuasive and emotional nature in a situation [. . .] which
requires a decision to be taken' (Maskell, p. 97). In *Phèdre*, as
elsewhere in Racine, it is the protagonists' expressive
exchanges (and occasional monologues) – tense, passionate,
touching, or bitter – which advance the action through their
power to sway judgement and resolve. The logic of the
protagonists' shifting emotions shapes the course of the
drama.

Hippolyte

Racine's Hippolyte appears at first as the affectionate and
admiring son of Thésée and his attitude towards Thésée illu-
minates his own character. For Thésée presents a 'macho
role-model' of heroic physical prowess and womanising.

Hippolyte is admiring of the first and responds idealistically to it, but considers the second debasing and unfeeling. Uneasy at Thésée's prolonged absence and at his own failure to take any action to bring him back, he is embarrassed by his tutor Théramène's suggestion that Thésée may be detained by an amorous entanglement. Hippolyte wants to believe that his father has left behind his errors and what he significantly calls Thésée's 'fateful inconstancy'. As for himself, he explains that his own disquiet results from the arrival in Troezen of Phèdre, but the explanation is oblique, for the real problem as he sees it is not his stepmother but the princess Aricie, the last of an enemy line, whom Phèdre has brought with her. There is irony here in that Phèdre is the true enemy and threat whereas Aricie is his destined partner until death. When Théramène rejoins that Aricie is innocent and that Hippolyte has no need to fear her, Hippolyte replies with a precious conceit – if he hated her, he would not be running away from her – which reveals the tone of their incipient relationship.

Théramène's gently ironic suggestion that Hippolyte is in love (lines 61–5) provokes Hippolyte to protest too much and too indignantly:

> Des sentiments d'un cœur si fier, si dédaigneux,
> Peux-tu me demander le désaveu honteux?
> C'est peu qu'avec son lait une mère amazone
> M'a fait sucer encor cet orgueil qui t'étonne.   (I.i.67)

(Can you ask me shamefully to disavow the feelings of such a proud disdainful heart as mine? I did not merely imbibe with my Amazonian mother's milk that pride that you wonder at.)

And he adds revealingly, and full of self-congratulation on the wisdom he has gained from experience (comic in one so young):

> Dans un âge plus mûr moi-même parvenu,
> Je me suis applaudi quand je me suis connu   (I.i.71)

(And I myself when more mature approved my nature when I knew myself)

Hippolyte means to say no more than that he is proud of his Amazonian origins. To the machismo that he has inherited from one side must be added the austere celibacy and cult of self-mastery which comes from the other. The embarrassing difficulty which Racine faces of making the misogynistic purity of the young hero acceptable to a seventeenth-century audience is solved by transforming him into a virginal discoverer of first love. But all his upbringing causes him to feel that this is a humiliating experience. He feels strongly that he has not proved the manhood which would compensate or excuse the indulgence of the weaker passion as it did in his father's case – a less noble concern than simply to prove himself (lines 98–100). And so he must banish all idea of going against his father's interdict on Aricie:

> Dois-je épouser ses droits contre un père irrité?
> Donnerai-je l'exemple à la témérité?
> Et dans un fol amour ma jeunesse embarquée ...   (I.i.111)

(Shall I espouse her cause against a father's wrath? Shall I set an example to foolhardiness? And engaging my youth in a wild passion ...)

Here, in his claim to wisdom and prudence, the primness of inexperience is very evident. The modulation of the intransigent puritan into the romantic lead is achieved very dexterously by Racine through a self-revelation provoked by teasing questioning suggestive of Marivaux.

Aricie's confidant, Ismène, is able to tell her that Hippolyte has a lover's eye, if not a lover's tongue (line 414), and Aricie responds to what she calls his 'orgueil généreux' (line 443) or noble pride, an expression with a Cornelian ring. Hippolyte is soon behaving like the courtly lover and continues to illustrate the precious conceit of the captive captor by executing a sentimental volte-face. Having, verbally at least, rejected not long since all suggestion of allowing himself to be an emotional captive of Aricie (line 95), he is now all concern for Aricie's freedom, ridding her of the tutelage formerly imposed by the supposedly dead Thésée, and handing back to her the right of succession (lines 474, 478). Like the eponymous hero of Thomas Corneille's *Timocrate* (1656), who, going out to battle, had fallen in love with the beautiful enemy queen, Hippolyte changes sides. He is now, like the lovelorn romantic,

'un prince déplorable' (line 529; a pitiable prince), 'Asservi
[. . .] sous la commune loi' (line 535; in bondage to the common
law), and describes himself in a manner reminiscent of the
ill-fated Oreste of *Andromaque* (lines 539–41). He no longer
recognises himself; he seeks but cannot find himself again (line
548). And, prophetically for the manner of his death, he has
neglected his horsemanship:

> Je ne me souviens plus des leçons de Neptune;
> Mes seuls gémissements font retentir les bois,
> Et mes coursiers oisifs ont oublié ma voix.   (II.ii.550)

(I no longer remember the lessons Neptune taught me. Only my
complaints now make the woods resound, and my idle steeds no
longer know my voice [Neptune, or in Greek Poseidon, supposedly
taught humans the art of breaking in horses].)

At all events, Racine has skilfully transformed the very stiff
and arrogant Hippolytus of Euripides and Seneca into a
young man smitten with a tender passion, appealing to men
and women of sensibility in the audience.

But something of the unreconstructed Hippolyte reappears
in confrontation with his unloved stepmother. He becomes
stiff and formal in response to her conciliatory overtures, and
has recourse to the kind of sententious utterance more
common in his predecessors ancient or modern:

> Des droits de ses enfants une mère jalouse
> Pardonne rarement au fils d'une autre épouse,
>   [. . .]Les soupçons importuns
> Sont d'un second hymen les fruits les plus communs
>
> (II.v.609)

(A mother jealous of her children's rights rarely forgives another
wife's son ... Constant suspicion is the commonest outcome of a
second marriage)

He is polite and uncomprehending, misunderstanding
Phèdre's state of mind and imagining that she is anxious about
the absence of Thésée. It hardly surprising that Hippolyte has
the greatest difficulty in believing that his stepmother could
have designs on him. The step-relationship alienates him,
independently of his attachment to Aricie, of which Phèdre is

not yet aware. She can understand Hippolyte's reaction only as that of a contempt for women which arouses her resentment. When Phèdre reveals her desire for him, Hippolyte is not only horrified by her, but horrified at himself, as if he himself were somehow defiled (lines 717–18). We are persuaded of the genuineness of Hippolyte's piety and moral integrity. The news that Phèdre's son is to be king, however, provokes from him an unprecedented and bitterly ironic complaint against the injustice of the gods:

> Dieux, qui la connaissez,
> Est-ce donc sa vertu que vous récompensez? (II.vi.727)

(O Gods, who know her, is it then her virtue that you are rewarding?)

Meeting Thésée, Hippolyte begs to be allowed to disappear for ever from the place where Phèdre lives (lines 925–6). With his father's return he is no longer responsible for the safety of Phèdre and Aricie, and he expresses a desire to do something more worthy than hunt wild animals. Clearly Hippolyte is still obsessed with his father's physical prowess and his own inadequacy. He longs to go off and kill any monster that remains in being and bring it back in glory – or die gloriously himself in the attempt. Faced with amorous entanglements, his thoughts turn once again to hunting and heroic pursuits. But there is no escape. Thésée voices the doubts that Phèdre has sown in his mind by speaking of an outrage done to him:

> Qui m'a trahi? Pourquoi ne suis-je pas vengé?
>
> Vous ne répondez point! Mon fils, mon propre fils
> Est-il d'intelligence avec mes ennemis? (III.v.980, 983)

(Who has betrayed me? Why am I not avenged? You do not answer. Is my son, my own son, colluding with my enemies?)

Appalled by Thésée's resolve to extract the truth from Phèdre, Hippolyte wonders anxiously what she will say. He reflects solemnly on the evil that love has brought to his father's house, but naively believes that in his innocence he himself has nothing to fear (lines 995–6). He concludes his soliloquy (III.vi) with scarcely justified hopefulness:

> Allons, cherchons ailleurs par quelle heureuse adresse
> Je pourrai de mon père émouvoir la tendresse,
> Et lui dire un amour qu'il peut vouloir troubler,
> Mais que tout son pouvoir ne saurait ébranler.   (III.vi.997)

(Come, let me seek some other happier device to awake my father's tenderness and tell him of a love he may wish to frustrate, but which it is not in his power to shake.)

Once again, Hippolyte is made to appeal to the audience through his sensibility, a quality which contrasts with the stiff dignity he displays in the tense confrontation which follows.

Stunned by the revelation that Phèdre accuses him of criminal designs on her, Hippolyte nevertheless refuses to reveal to Thésée what he knows of Phèdre's feelings (lines 1089–90). But this inevitably provokes Thésée to challenge him to explain and defend himself and a heated exchange follows. The lofty and sententious Hippolyte reappears:

> Examinez ma vie, et songez qui je suis.
> Quelques crimes toujours précèdent les grands crimes.
> (IV.ii.1092)

(Examine my life, remember who I am. Great crimes are always preceded by lesser ones.)

His assertion that he does not seek to paint himself in too favourable a light (line 1105) verges on self-righteousness, but the famous line of monsyllables: 'Le jour n'est pas plus pur que le fond de mon cœur' (line 1112; Day is not purer than my inmost heart) carries immediate conviction of its sincerity and truth.

In these bitter exchanges between Thésée and Hippolyte, imitated from Euripides, the French is more decorous, less savage than the Greek, and although Thésée is scarcely less contemptuous, Hippolyte is less the adversary in debate, reproaching his father for excess of forensic cleverness, than he is constantly dignified and restrained, sustained by a sense of his own integrity.

Racine introduces Hippolyte's relationship with Aricie into the debate with great adroitness. For the prime charge levelled against Euripides' Hippolytus by his father is that of hypocrisy: false claims to chastity concealing lechery. Hippolyte's confession of his love for Aricie is treated analogously: lust, so Thésée claims, is being hypocritically concealed beneath a specious cloak of tender feeling for a rival to the throne; the lesser crime is confessed to in order to disguise the greater.

Hippolyte's restraint nevertheless finally snaps under Thésée's sustained invective, and he alludes obliquely to his stepmother's tainted ancestry. Thereby he seals his fate. The accusation is more hurtful to his father than the resentment of his bastardy expressed by the Hippolytus of Euripides. Hippolyte's loss of self-control under intense pressure is psychologically true and more plausible (although not more dramatic) than the intellectual debate between father and son in Euripides, which, like so much of the haughty dialectic of the Greek, would be more at home in Corneille.

In his exchanges with Aricie in the last act, Hippolyte is once again an appealing figure. Pressed to defend himself against Thésée's charge, he remains unwilling to speak out publicly and cause his father pain (line 1340). There is a pathetic sincerity in his cry to Aricie:

> Mon cœur pour s'épancher n'a que vous et les dieux
>
> (V.i.1344)

(Would I pour out my heart, I have only you and the gods)

And, ironically, he still puts his trust in the gods (lines 1351–2). But they have conflicting interests, and their concern for Hippolyte has thus far been invisible.

At this point, Hippolyte resolves upon political action – not quite what one might have expected from a character who hitherto has spent his time hunting or pining; but in falling in love with Aricie and promising to restore her right to the throne he has made for himself a political ally. In mingling love and politics, Racine follows the mainstream of seventeenth-century French serious drama. Aricie is urged to flee with Hippolyte and league with him against Phèdre to foil attempts to place Phèdre's son on the throne. This is a call to arms, almost a set piece, a proud passage of rhetorical assessment of their chances in a battle for supremacy:

De puissants défenseurs prendront notre querelle,
Argos nous tend les bras, et Sparte nous appelle;
A nos amis communs portons nos justes cris,
Ne souffrons pas que Phèdre, assemblant nos débris,
Du trône paternel nous chasse l'un et l'autre,
Et promette à son fils ma dépouille et la vôtre.
L'occasion est belle, il la faut embrasser ...   (V.i.1365)

(Mighty defenders will take up our cause; Argos opens its arms, Sparta calls us. Let us carry our just grievances to our common friends. Let us not allow Phèdre to assemble the remnants of our domains and drive us both from my father's throne, stripping us of our inheritance in favour of her son. Now is our great chance. We must grasp it ...)

Yet Aricie holds back. Hippolyte is disconcerted. He chides her in a line which gives to the Petrarchan commonplace of the ardent lover and the cold beloved an urgent practical meaning: 'Quand je suis tout de feu, d'où vous vient cette glace?' (line 1374; When I am all ardour, why are you so cold?). For the ardour of the lover is for immediate departure to pursue a political purpose, and the coldness of the loved one is not a supercilious pose designed to test the lover's constancy, but the result of her fear that Hippolyte will not await the marriage ceremony before possessing her. 'The height of virtuous insipidity', in Thierry Maulnier's view (*Lecture de Phèdre* (1943) (Paris, 1967), p.106), yet it is of a piece with the touching purity of Hippolyte. Belief in the chastity of Hippolyte and Aricie is as necessary to Racine's tragedy as belief in the puritanical piety of Hippolytus is to that of Euripides. And to an audience whose culture was Christian, the sentiments of the two lovers were certainly more immediately intelligible than those of the mythical Greek. But clearly in both cases the characters must be understood in their context and through the conventions, and the language of the conventions, that obtain. Racine has a remarkable gift of conferring conviction and vitality on the commonplaces of preciosity and sensibility. Hippolyte now believes that his and Aricie's destiny is to be free: 'Libres dans nos malheurs, puisque le ciel l'ordonne' (line 1389; Free in our misfortunes, since heaven orders it so). The formula is full of a profound unconscious irony. Hippolyte promises in a touchingly lyrical passage to pledge his faith before all the gods (lines 1403–6) but the gods will destroy him before his vows can be made.

Hippolyte's last words, quoted by Théramène in his messenger speech, are to recommend Aricie to his father's care (lines 1565–7). Death overtakes him before he can complete his plea.

Racine's Hippolyte is clearly a more complex figure than his Greek model. He has a different rôle in a different play. The Greek Hippolytus is a pawn in the hands of the gods as much as his stepmother is and the play illustrates and exemplifies the powers of those gods. Hippolytus' puritanical devotion to Artemis is complicated only by his resented illegitimacy, which partly explains his misogyny – although hardly with good reason – and is aggravated by his resentment of his stepmother, who has a legitimate son of her own. Racine's Hippolyte is an outdoor sportsman, a would-be slayer of dragons, an idealist with a cult of self-mastery, suspicious of women, alienated from his stepmother, a romantic lover and man of sensibility, a political strategist rebelling against an admired and loved but unjust father. These things are not inherently incompatible, and certainly they are not so in Racine, but Hippolyte is too complicated to be the incarnation of a particular credo or ideology. He is, however, well suited to the role of victim of the relentless contrivances of an inescapable fate.

Phèdre

Racine's play begins like Euripides' by presenting Hippolyte to the audience. Phèdre appears with Œnone in the third scene of the play, weak and trembling, oppressed by her clothing and jewellery. Both she and Œnone speak of her hatred for the light of day and Phèdre utters the ominous line: 'Soleil, je te viens voir pour la dernière fois!' (line 172; O Sun, for the last time I come to look on you). The sun, from which Phèdre is descended, stands for some unclearly defined principle of justice or 'rightness'.

As in Euripides, Phèdre expresses a longing or nostalgia for life in the countryside and, more surprisingly, a desire to join the hunt, which is Hippolyte's domain. The nurse, in reproaching her for yielding to despair, and in attempting to assign a reason for her depression, mentions Hippolyte (lines 203–5). The horror-struck reaction that this produces in Phèdre: 'Malheureuse, quel nom est sorti de ta bouche?' (line 206; Wretch, what name has passed your lips?) at once suggests the source of Phèdre's distress. But she manifests a deep reluctance to reveal her passion, indeed would rather die than do so (line 226). Like Euripides' Phaedra, she believes that to confess an illicit passion would be to stain her honour and make her more culpable. Again as in Euripides' Phaedra, her thoughts turn to the perverted love of her mother for the bull (lines 249–50), and the theme of the divine curse on Phèdre's family is introduced for the first time.

Phèdre explains in one of her most gripping speeches that it is not merely since her arrival in Troezen that she has fallen in love with Hippolyte: 'Mon mal vient de plus loin' (line 269; My sickness started long before ['plus loin' can also refer to physical distance; the word 'mal' can also mean sorrow, pain, or evil]). There is something ominous about the vague but evocative opening. The distant origin of her malady is however at once made known. She fell in love with Hippolyte in Athens soon after her marriage. Her highly charged account of her feelings on seeing Hippolyte is physical in its eroticism, perhaps more directly sensual than other evocations of the passion of love in Racine. Even so, it would not have seemed out of place in *L'Astrée*, that early seventeenth-century French romance which sought to spiritualise physical love. In a passage evocative of Virgil's Dido (*Aeneid*, 4.62–6), Phèdre speaks of building a temple to Venus and making sacrifices to no avail, since the god she really worships is Hippolyte. She tries to avoid him but finds him pictured in his father's features. Phèdre both believes her passion to be inflicted by a god, and tries to avoid the occasion of the sin to which it prompts.

From the evocation of physical passion, Phèdre passes to an

account of her efforts to distance herself from Hippolyte by coldness, by driving him into exile, but his return arouses the old fire: 'C'est Vénus tout entière à sa proie attachée' (line 306; Venus in all her might grasping her prey) – a line expressively adapted from Horace (*Odes*, 1.19.9). But her efforts to escape are redoubled this time by her resolve to die and so save her reputation: 'Je voulais en mourant prendre soin de ma gloire' (line 309; I wanted in dying to preserve my great name).

Racine presents his themes more briefly than Euripides. A few lines evoke the power and persecution of Venus, a few words speak of Phèdre's sense of shame. In Euripides the goddess Aphrodite appears at the outset to express her designs on the characters so that the supernatural source of Phaedra's passion is well established. What has so far been conveyed most powerfully in Racine is the sheer sensual intensity of Phèdre's passion and the unsparing efforts she makes to resist it. She seems to believe in the possibility of controlling it. She confesses therefore to Œnone on condition that the nurse abandons all attempts to revive what Phèdre describes as the remains of a passion on the point of expiring. But this is wishful thinking.

A dramatic reversal of situation comes with the announcement of the death of Thésée. Phèdre's love for Hippolyte might now according to Œnone be considered innocent. The nurse urges Phèdre to join with Hippolyte against Aricie – a dramatic irony – in order to preserve her own son. This makes a sentimental appeal to the audience. Four scenes devoted to Hippolyte and Aricie intervene before Phèdre comes on stage again to confront Hippolyte. In this scene Phèdre is concerned, after Œnone's warning, to conciliate Hippolyte and save her son, but in apologising for her coldness towards Hippolyte, she slides into revealing her feelings for him. Her previous confession to Œnone that she could not help seeing Hippolyte's image in the features of his father is confirmed in reverse when she meets Hippolyte again and sees his father's likeness in him: 'Que dis-je? Il n'est point mort puisqu'il respire en vous' (line 627; What am I saying? He is not dead since he lives in you). She is soon carried away: 'Oui

Prince, je languis, je brûle pour Thésée' (line 634; Yes, Prince, I pine, I am on fire for Thésée).

The erotic fantasy is not in Euripides. It is indebted to Seneca, but Seneca's Phaedra is more pitiable, Racine's more sensual. Euripides' heroine is nobler, she preserves her royal dignity as Racine's Phèdre does not or cannot. But Phèdre pulls herself up briefly – perhaps Racine remembers his Euripides – when Hippolyte asks whether she has forgotten that Thésée is her husband and Hipppolyte's father:

> Et sur quoi jugez-vous que j'en perds la mémoire,
> Prince? Aurais-je perdu tout le soin de ma gloire?   (II.v.665)

(What makes you think, Prince, that I have forgotten? Could I have lost all concern for my great name?)

It is hard to say whether Phèdre's concern for her 'gloire' is more or less a principle of caste, more or less a moral principle, than the concern of Euripides' Phaedra for her good reputation. Euripides' Phaedra moralises more extensively than Racine's, but the French heroine's sense of sin is as marked as that of the Greek heroine.

Certainly the outburst which follows expresses a strong sense of self-condemnation:

> J'aime. Ne pense pas qu'au moment que je t'aime,
> Innocente à mes yeux, je m'approuve moi-même,
> Ni que du fol amour qui trouble ma raison,
> Ma lâche complaisance ait nourri le poison.   (II.v.673)

(I am in love. Do not suppose that in loving you I approve what I feel, nor think that a weak indulgence has fed the poison of the frenzied love that distracts my mind.)

And Phèdre's sense of subjection to forces beyond her control becomes a bitter complaint against the gods (lines 677–82). It seems not that a particular god is persecuting Phèdre, but that the gods collectively are against her. In her passionate exchange with Hippolyte, she points to her desperate attempts to conquer her passion for him and her failure to resist it. Even her confession to him is involuntary. Racine effects a deft transition from her complaint against persecution by the gods to her expression of helplessness to resist Hippolyte's charms when in his presence:

> Tremblante pour un fils que je n'osais trahir,
> Je te venais prier de ne le point haïr.
> Faibles projets d'un cœur trop plein de ce qu'il aime!
> Hélas! je ne t'ai pu parler que de toi-même.   (II.v.695)

(Fearing for a son whom I dared not betray, I wanted to beg you not to hate him – such was the feeble plan of a heart too full of what it loves! Alas! I could speak to you only of yourself!)

Fate and psychological determinism become indistinguishable.

Phèdre condemns herself as a monster of which Hippolyte is best suited to rid the universe, following the example of his father, the slayer of monsters. She reaches the depth of that self-loathing and self-rejection which will determine her death in the final scene of the play. There is a marked contrast with Seneca's Phaedra, who is essentially pitiful and submissive, eager to perish by Hippolyte's sword and die with her honour intact. Œnone's suggested remedy for Phèdre's plight is political: to abandon thoughts of Hippolyte and ascend the throne. For this Phèdre has no longer the strength or the resolution (lines 759–80). There is no going back, for Phèdre has uttered words that should never have been spoken (line 742) and overstepped the bounds of strict modesty (line 766).

Yet, contrary to what follows in Euripides and Seneca, Phèdre's confession of love encourages hope of requital (lines 767–8). Œnone is blamed, nonetheless, for reviving Phèdre's feelings for Hippolyte; and, from arguing for an alliance with Hippolyte now that Thésée is supposedly dead, she is impelled by Hippolyte's rebuff to advise against Phèdre's having any relation with him, citing the familiar obstacle of his misogyny. The reversals of the plot cause Phèdre's attitudes to Hippolyte to oscillate, and her hopes of attracting him to rise and fall. To these oscillations Œnone has to accommodate herself in her turn.

A tide of wishful thinking carries Phèdre away. Perhaps Hippolyte's resistance is simply a result of his rustic way of life and unfamiliarity with the sentiments of love? To Œnone's categorical 'Il a pour tout le sexe une haine fatale' (line 789; He hates all women with a deadly hate), she retorts with emotional logic, or illogic, 'Je ne me verrai point préférer de rivale' (line 790; No rival will be preferred to me). There is a deep irony in this. She even explicitly rejects logic in her exchanges with Œnone:

> Enfin tous ces conseils ne sont plus de saison:
> Sers ma fureur, Œnone, et non point ma raison.   (III.i.791)

(In short, all such good advice is no longer timely; serve my wild passion, Œnone, and not my reason.)

But paradoxically, having previously rejected Œnone's political advice to seize power, on the grounds that she is no longer mistress of her reason, she now proposes her own plan of offering Hippolyte an alliance. Clearly this is a policy calculated to suit her passion. She rests her hopes on Hippolyte, seeing him as a possible substitute father for her son, rather than as his rival. Once again this makes an appeal to sentiment in the audience. She surrenders completely to her feelings for Hippolyte and commits her fate into the hands of the previously reviled Œnone (lines 810–12).

But there is yet another reversal in this complicated plot. Thésée returns, and the distraught Phèdre once again blames Œnone for the impossible predicament in which she now finds herself (lines 837–8). For she now fears the humiliation of finding her feelings revealed by Hippolyte, who, she is convinced, could not conceal his horror of her even if he tried. Phèdre here professes the same sense of shame and concern for her reputation that are shown by Euripides' heroine:

> Je ne crains que le nom que je laisse après moi.
> Pour mes tristes enfants quel affreux héritage!   (III.iii.860)

(I fear only for the name I leave behind me. What an appalling legacy for my poor children!)

But the Greek heroine was consistent, and Phèdre continues to vacillate. When asked by Œnone how she now feels about Hippolyte, she replies that she sees him as a fearful monster (line 884). Œnone's response is to propose that she should accuse him first of outrageous behaviour. Phèdre's shocked reply: 'Moi, que j'ose opprimer et noircir l'innocence!' (line 893; That I should dare to oppress and blacken innocence!) is met by Œnone's: 'Mon zèle n'a besoin que de votre silence' (line 894; All I need to succeed is your silence). Œnone, it turns out, knows her mistress well, for, catching sight of Hippolyte entering with Thésée, Phèdre fears the worst and yields to Œnone:

> Fais ce que tu voudras, je m'abandonne à toi.
> Dans le trouble où je suis, je ne puis rien pour moi.
>
> (III.iii.911)

(Do as you will. I abandon myself to you. In my distraught state I can do nothing for myself.)

These are particularly telling lines for the assessment of Phèdre's responsibility for Hippolyte's fate.

Phèdre's reception of the returning Thésée is ingeniously equivocal, and it is not easy to say whether the ingenuity of formulation should be taken to reveal disingenuousness or (as in Seneca) a state of desperation. The two are not, of course, mutually exclusive states of mind.

> Vous êtes offensé. La fortune jalouse
> N'a pas en votre absence épargné votre épouse.
> Indigne de vous plaire et de vous approcher,
> Je ne dois désormais songer qu'à me cacher.   (III.iv.917)

(You are insulted. Jealous fortune has not spared your wife during your absence. I am unworthy to approach or please you. My only thought henceforth must be to hide myself.)

In Phèdre's own mind this could indeed be an expression of her own sense of guilt at her illicit passion, but it can only arouse Thésée's suspicions that an outrage has been committed upon Phèdre herself. When Thésée pronounces his curse on Hippolyte, Phèdre begs him to relent. But Thésée's quite casual mention, in reply, of Hippolyte's confession of his love for Aricie provokes yet another volte-face. In the jealous soliloquy which fills Act IV, scene v, Phèdre repents bitterly of the sympathy for Hippolyte to which she had yielded (lines 1199–200, 1207–8, 1212–13).

Her jealousy is expressed with peculiar bitterness and violence in her exchanges with Œnone in IV.vi, a scene of long and passionate speeches largely analysed in an earlier section (see 'Language'). What particularly embitters Phèdre is the contrast between the innocence of the love between Aricie and Hippolyte and her own guilty passion (lines 1238, 1241–2). Self-pity generates a desire for revenge (lines 1258–60), but is followed immediately by her appalled recognition of the sheer irrationality of her looking to Thésée to revenge her on her rival in love – for presenting an obstacle to her adulterous desires – and the tirade ends in self-condemnation (lines 1264–5, 1273–4).

This has been an extraordinary and indeed bewildering succession of oscillations between attraction to Hippolyte and revulsion from him. One may ask whether Phèdre has undergone all these changes of attitude freely, or whether or how far they can be attributed to the work of the gods, who are intermittently referred to. If we suppose that the action as a whole is under their control, we must take it that the apparent freedom of Phèdre is illusory and itself a product of divine agency. But the picture as we have it is of a character impelled by a passion of which she cannot rid herself, yet having the power to react to it in various ways and seemingly bearing the responsibility for her reactions.

Œnone seeks to comfort her with the observation that there is nothing extraordinary or shocking about being carried away by the passion of love: Phèdre has simply followed her destiny (lines 1297–8). But this provokes an explosion of moral denunciation from Phèdre, who holds Œnone ultimately responsible for her crime:

> Puisse le juste ciel dignement te payer;
> Et puisse ton supplice à jamais effrayer
> Tous ceux qui, comme toi, par de lâches adresses,
> Des princes malheureux nourrissent les faiblesses,
> Les poussent au penchant où leur cœur est enclin,
> Et leur osent du crime aplanir le chemin!   (IV.vi.1319)

(May the just heavens reward you fittingly, and may your punishment for ever frighten all who, as you have done, by base devices foster ill-fated princes' weaknesses, urging them to yield to the temptation to which they incline, and daring to smooth for them the path of crime!)

Princes, then, so this speciously sententious argument implies, are much less to blame for yielding to their own weaknesses if their advisers have given them encouragement to do so. Phèdre certainly exaggerates Œnone's responsibility and plays down her own in asserting that:

> Le ciel mit dans mon sein une flamme funeste;
> La détestable Œnone a conduit tout le reste.   (V.vii.1625)

(Heaven lit an ill-omened flame in my heart; hateful Œnone plotted all the rest.)

For Œnone was blind to the disaster for which she was preparing the way by persuading Phèdre to avoid Hippolyte no longer, and both she and Phèdre were ignorant of the relationship between Hippolyte and Aricie, knowledge of which was to prove so destructive to Phèdre. Only in the last lines of her speech does Phèdre finally express, as she dies, a recognition of the extent of her own guilt (lines 1643–4).

In the end, Phèdre appears less the innocent victim than the subject of a profound moral ambivalence, bordering on the pathological. Phèdre, after all, is a sick woman, perhaps delirious in Racine as in Euripides. Lustful, jealous, self-deceiving and conscience-stricken, exhausted and bewildered by her own conflicting emotions and the twists and turns of fate, she is truly the 'weak mortal' that she claims to be.

Œnone

Œnone as her mistress's former nurse is assigned the status of confidant in Racine's play, but her influence on her mistress's conduct and on others' understanding of it makes her role in the action of the play a crucial one.

What is first drawn to our attention is her concern for her mistress's well-being, when she reports to Hippolyte that: 'Elle meurt dans mes bras d'un mal qu'elle me cache' (line 146; She is dying in my arms from a malady which she is hiding from me). Racine follows Euripides in representing the nurse as scolding Phèdre for her silence. Much more succinct than her Euripidean counterpart, Œnone employs the same arguments against Phèdre offending the gods and her husband, thereby putting her own son at risk from the son of the Amazon. Œnone's attempts to calm Phèdre's fears and her horror at hearing that Phèdre is in love with Hippolyte also follow Euripides. Unlike Seneca's nurse, Œnone does not reject her mistress's claim that her passion has been inflicted by the gods.

The report of Thésée's death naturally causes Œnone to change her advice. Better for Phèdre to find a protector for her son by allying herself with Hippolyte than offend him by an appearance of aversion. The advice is sound and responsible as is all her advice at this stage. When Phèdre has incontinently declared her passion to Hippolyte, and, on his rejecting her, challenged him to run her through with his sword, Œnone suggests that Phèdre should seize the throne, or if she does not feel capable of doing so, flee Hippolyte. Her reminder to Phèdre of Hippolyte's arrogant demeanour towards women is entirely justified. Phèdre, however, holds Œnone responsible for reviving her hopes of attracting Hippolyte's affections (line 772) – which is true enough, but fails to excuse her own lack of caution and restraint. Œnone's rhetorical question:

> Hélas! de vos malheurs innocente ou coupable,
> De quoi pour vous sauver n'étais-je point capable?

> (III.i.773)

(Alas! guilty or not of your misfortunes, what would I not have been capable of to save your life?)

without admitting responsibility so far, reveals her readiness to resort to deviousness in the future. It is when Phèdre threatens to kill herself at the news that Thésée has returned, reproaching the nurse once again with having dissuaded her from dying with honour, that Œnone makes her proposal that Phèdre should accuse Hippolyte before he accuses her.

In accusing Hippolyte of rape, Œnone, like Seneca's nurse,

behaves much more criminally than does Euripides' nurse in
revealing Phaedra's passion to Hippolytus. But Œnone's lapse
into criminality is much less of a volte-face, much less abrupt
than that of Seneca's nurse, for Œnone has made three quite
proper suggestions of ways of escape from Phèdre's difficulties
before she finally has recourse to criminal advice as a last
resort to save Phèdre from suicide. Phèdre cannot escape
blame by having left responsibility for the accusation to
Œnone, or by replying equivocally to Thésée when he urges
her to explain her distraught state. Racine both offers some
excuse for Œnone's action and allows Phèdre to equivocate
over her own responsibility. Œnone eventually brings her false
accusation against Hippolyte in an exchange with Thésée. She
explains Phèdre's silence on what had happened as arising
from a concern to spare the feelings of a father. Œnone
maintains that she has saved Phèdre for her husband's love by
dissuading her from committing suicide (lines 1019–20). And
she goes so far as to explain Phèdre's earlier coldness towards
Hippolyte in Athens as a reaction to his criminal love for her
(lines 1029–30). She claims disingenuously to have told Thésée
all that has passed (line 1032).

When, finally, Phèdre has been totally demoralised by the
news that she has a rival in Aricie, and by the recognition of
the madness of her own murderous reaction, she is once again
met with specious arguments of Œnone's defending the natur-
alness of moral weakness in human beings and citing the
examples of the illicit amours of the gods. After Phèdre's
formidable denunciation and rejection, Œnone assents rue-
fully to the accusation:

> Ah! Dieux! pour la servir j'ai tout fait, tout quitté;
> Et j'en reçois ce prix? Je l'ai bien mérité.   (IV.vi.1327)

(Ah Gods! to serve her I have done everything, given up everything;
and this is the reward that I receive? I have richly deserved it.)

Whether she really deserved the rejection is open to question.
Œnone, too, is a morally ambiguous character. She can,
however, be said to have brought the disaster upon herself,
and her reflection is a bitter one.

Œnone and Phèdre are characters involved in a kind of symbiotic relationship whose outcome must be common to both. They are portrayed sliding into criminality under the influence of powerful emotions, whether lust or personal devotion (Œnone furnishes an exception to the egoism of the Racinian ruling passion). The tracing of the stages by which they fall into error enables the audience to sympathise with them. Both are tragic figures. Their double suicide fulfils their joint destiny.

Aricie

Racine's borrowing from the ancient sequel to the Hippolytus legend, giving to Hippolyte a lover and to Phèdre a rival, contributes to the audience-appeal of the play and to the plausibility of the characterisation of Hippolyte in seventeenth-century French terms, and makes more credible and more powerful the intensity of Phèdre's tragic passion. It also gives a political dimension to the tragedy, introducing illusory suggestions of escape by political action from a predicament whose tragic outcome is inevitable. Aricie adds to the complexity of the plot and the added complexity increases the sense of a malignant fate which causes all human plans to go awry.

When, early in the play, Aricie learns that Hippolyte wishes to see her, she can hardly believe her ears, and is clearly flattered. She displays, however, the aristocratic haughtiness that we associate with the heroes and heroines of classical French tragedy, and with the heroine of the novel of preciosity whose lover has to prove himself by enduring the *rigueurs* of the beloved. Aricie's aristocratic poise and confidence remind us rather of figures from earlier in the century and before the heroic ethos had begun to lose its authority. Aricie is in fact attracted by the haughtiness of Hippolyte:

> J'aime, je l'avouerai, cet orgueil généreux
> Qui jamais n'a fléchi sous le joug amoureux.   (II.i.443)

(I love, I will confess, that noble pride, which has never bowed beneath love's yoke.)

But she sees it as a pride to be humbled:

> Mais de faire fléchir un courage inflexible,
> De porter la douleur dans une âme insensible,
> D'enchaîner un captif de ses fers étonné,
> Contre un joug qui lui plaît vainement mutiné,
> C'est là ce que je veux, c'est là ce qui m'irrite.   (II.i.449)

(But to make an unbending spirit yield, to cause pain in an unfeeling heart, to chain a captive astonished by his fetters and in vain rebelling against a pleasing yoke, that is what I want, that is what I find challenging.)

This might have presaged a tense relationship. But the characteristic Racinian note of self-pity has also been sounded in this exchange with her confidant:

> O toi qui me connais, te semblait-il croyable
> Que le triste jouet d'un sort impitoyable,
> Un cœur toujours nourri d'amertume et de pleurs,
> Dût connaître l'amour et ses folles douleurs?   (II.i.417)

(O you who know me, did it seem credible to you that the sad plaything of a pitiless fate, a heart always fed on bitterness and tears, should ever know love and its wild sufferings?)

Aricie is haughty, romantic and pitiful all at once, an infallible formula for charming the seventeenth-century audience, and indeed the modern audience, if it will allow itself to be charmed. Her response to Hippolyte's expression of readiness to revoke all restrictions on her freedom (line 475) is at first to receive it with reserve as a form of condescension or of indirect dominance (lines 481–4), but her final words to Hippolyte are grateful and melting (lines 572–6).

After these first three scenes of Act II, Aricie does not appear again until the first three scenes of Act V. But her potential political role, which Hippolyte is the first to wish to exploit, plays in the interval an important part in influencing the plans and decisions of Phèdre and Œnone, creating suspense and prolonging plausibly the fruitless efforts of the protagonists to escape their fate.

In Act II, Aricie was encouraging Hippolyte to agree to his stepmother's request to talk to him observing that he owed some sympathy at least to Phèdre's tears. When Aricie next appears, in the last act, Phèdre has allowed Hippolyte to be condemned for rape, and Aricie is now concerned to urge him not to protect his stepmother at the expense of his own reputation, but to defend himself against Thésée's condemnation. The attitudes of Hippolyte and Aricie have become reversed. Aricie is particularly distressed by the thought that Hippolyte may be leaving her. His proposal that they should flee Troezen together and seek allies elsewhere against Phèdre and Thésée is accepted eagerly once she is reassured that they will take solemn marriage vows. Thésée's heavily ironic reference to Hippolyte's 'respect' for women transposes something of the bitter exchanges between Theseus and the dying Hippolytus in Euripides, and provokes a formidable denunciation of Phèdre from Aricie in which she is on the point of characterising Phèdre herself as a monster whom Thésée omitted to destroy. Only Hippolyte's example restrains her from speaking plainly. Aricie's powerful speech serves to awaken Thésée's misgivings and to prompt in him thoughts of extracting the truth from the nurse (Seneca's Theseus had had similar thoughts). But Œnone is dead, and Hippolyte's fate is certain. Aricie does not come on stage again, but the pathos of her bereavement is conveyed in speeches of other characters, notably that of Théramène (lines 1574–88).

Aricie, although clearly a figure constructed according to seventeenth-century French conventions and introduced to solve the problem of characterisation presented by the outlandishly virginal figure of Hippolytus, has a vital role in determining the thoughts and actions of other characters, and if she brings charm and delicate pathos to her role, her personality is not without force.

Thésée

Thésée is the very type of the tragic hero: a false move made in anger destroys a son he deeply loved and plunges him into unassuageable grief. So he appears in Euripides and Seneca. The Greek and Roman authors make a markedly rhetorical and emotional appeal in their different ways. Euripides' Theseus engages in moral, philosophical, and religious debate on a lofty plane. Seneca's offers us towering speeches of lament. Racine is clearly concerned with Thésée's role in the action. Whatever is taken over or imitated from his classical predecessors is condensed. Racine applies himself to creating suspense, curiosity, and peripeteia. Thésée has repeated exchanges with other main characters which contribute to the action of the play. Whereas in the Greek and Roman authors he appears in three or four long scenes, in Racine he appears in a dozen scenes, sometimes very brief, sometimes consisting of short soliloquies (often corresponding functionally to longer speeches in the ancient plays), but helping the action onwards.

Racine's Thésée returns to Troezen to be at once confronted with a mystery. His expressions of pleasure at rejoining his wife are cut short by her withdrawal amid ominous expressions of her own unworthiness. Turning to Hippolyte, he encounters similar evasions and a desire for death with honour. He is bewildered and pleads for explanation (lines 953–4). He is met with Phèdre's assertion that an outrage has been committed against him (line 979). Doubts are sown in his mind about the loyalty of his son and he resolves to interrogate Phèdre and ascertain the truth. This legendary hero is a man of integrity and a lover of his family, but given to quick and decisive reactions rather than cautious reflection. It is this that will be his undoing.

Œnone's denunciation of Hippolyte produces an outburst of indignation from Thésée (lines 1001–13) and some rash and prejudiced interpretations of Hippolyte's reactions to his previous questioning of him (lines 1023–8). This has the effect of allowing Œnone to evade awkward questions about Phèdre's relations with Hippolyte. Consequently, in the following exchange with Hippolyte, Thésée has no hesitation in addressing him with the contemptuous irony employed by the Theseus of Euripides. In a resounding passage of denunciation ending with his pronouncing banishment, Thésée calls down on his son the wrath of Neptune who has promised to execute

Thésée's wishes. Prone as he is to precipitate judgement and uncontrolled rage, Thésée cannot believe Hippolyte to be sincere in his expression of love for Aricie, only cunningly fraudulent. Hippolyte's final loss of patience and his allusion to Phèdre's guilty heredity proves the last straw, and, given Thésée's ignorance, the first justifiable pretext for his anger. The short soliloquy of Thésée's which follows is an emotional high point in which Thésée confirms his condemnation of his son, but admits that some love for him remains. At a moment of high emotion, contradictory feelings mingle.

The subsequent scene, IV.iv, in which Phèdre learns from Thésée that he has called on Neptune to destroy Hippolyte and of Hippolyte's love for Aricie, is introduced for the dramatic impact it has on the state of mind of Phèdre. Thésée is merciless here in his determination to revenge himself on his son. But his appeal to the gods in V.ii and his interview with Aricie in V.iii bring to the fore the unease which has nevertheless affected him ever since his angry exchanges with Hippolyte:

> Dieux! éclairez mon trouble, et daignez à mes yeux
> Montrer la vérité, que je cherche en ces lieux!   (V.ii.1411)

(O Gods! enlighten my confusion and deign to reveal the truth that I am seeking here!)

His renewed sarcasms at Hippolyte's expense (lines 1422–4) and his emphatic – overemphatic – assertions of the 'incontrovertible' evidence of his wife's tears (lines 1441–2) cannot still the inner doubts evoked by Aricie's protestations of Hippolyte's innocence and her scarcely veiled accusations of Phèdre's role in the incident. Another monologue of Thésée's forms Act V, scene iv, at first an expression of doubt, uncertainty, and anguish concerning the sincerity of Aricie's claims, but soon allowing his natural feelings of pity for his son to well up again:

> Mais moi-même, malgré ma sévère rigueur,
> Quelle plaintive voix crie au fond de mon cœur?
> Une pitié secrète et m'afflige et m'étonne.   (V.iv.1455)

(But, for myself, despite my stern severity, what plaintive voice cries out in my inmost heart? A secret pity troubles and confounds me.)

By now (V.v) it is too late. The death of Œnone (line 1466) and the distraught state of Phèdre (lines 1469–79) cause him to repent of his appeal to Neptune, which he recognises to have been rash and prompted by doubtful testimony (lines 1485–6). His judgement is now the reverse of that he had previously expressed. Théramène's account of his son's death (V.vi) leaves him devastated:

> Inexorables dieux, qui m'avez trop servi!
> A quels mortels regrets ma vie est réservée!   (V.vi.1572)

(Inexorable Gods, who have served me all too well! To what deadly remorse my life is now destined!)

The final scene with Phèdre (V.vii) reveals the great and redoubtable hero, formerly resolved to seek out the truth, reduced to fleeing from it:

> Confus, persécuté d'un mortel souvenir,
> De l'univers entier je voudrais me bannir.   (V.vii.1607)

(Bewildered and harassed by this grim memory, I wish I could exile myself from the whole universe.)

He hates the gods and their favours and wishes he had not been a famous hero, unable to escape attention (lines 1611–12). By a cruel irony it is Phèdre who insists on revealing the truth of her guilt, expiating her crime at the expense of Thésée's last shreds of comfort. The state of dereliction in which he finds himself as a result of his rashly uttered curse imparts to his role a quality of tragic pathos comparable with that of Phèdre herself.

Ending

The tragic action of Racine's play comes to an end with the dying speech of Phèdre, but this has been preceded by the long speech of Théramène recounting the manner of Hippolyte's death. In the *Hippolytus* of Euripides, the hero dies in consequence of the curse that Theseus pronounces upon him following Phaedra's suicide, but the play concludes with the grand moral and religious debate between the dying Hippolytus and Theseus – and indeed Artemis. The messenger's account of the death of Hippolytus consequently becomes the occasion or the trigger of that debate, rather than the source of tragic emotion in itself. It is necessary and inevitable that Hippolytus should die; not necessary that the manner of his death should be elaborately narrated. But the messenger's speech has served as a model, a challenge, an opportunity too attractive to be missed by Euripides' imitators, Seneca and Racine. In Seneca it is massively elaborated as picturesque and macabre description. In Racine, closer to Euripides, it is characteristically more restrained and decorous. In postponing Phaedra's suicide until after she hears of Hippolytus' appalling death, Seneca displays a certain logic, which Racine only half follows, since his Phèdre takes her slow-acting poison before she learns of Hippolyte's death. But if in Euripides the narrative of the hero's death can be thought to be elaborated beyond what is required by its role or function in his play, the same might be said with apparently greater force of the corresponding messenger speeches in the plays of Seneca and Racine, which, essentially, are the tragedies not of Hippolytus, but of Phaedra. In Seneca the concern for effect is dominant, but in Racine bravura is rare. His 'récit de Théramène' has nevertheless continued to provoke conflicting opinions since its first appearance.

Racine's 'récit' extends to seventy-three lines – comparable to the eighty-one devoted to the corresponding speech by Euripides. Only one line is given to the geographical setting prominent in Euripides, but to the weeping of Hippolytus and his companions at the prospect of exile corresponds the dejection of Hippolyte and his horses in Racine. Racine's passage has a certain solemnity, as if foreshadowing the grim events to come. Perhaps the inclusion of the horses in the dejected mood anticipates their own approaching disaster. In Euripides, the horses are involved, rather, in the bustle of preparations for departure. But Racine passes quickly to the intervention of the monster. Euripides had written: 'a rumbling deep in the earth, dreadful to hear, growled like the thunder of Zeus' (lines 1201–3). Racine, however, speaks of:

> Un effroyable cri, sorti du fond des flots
>
> Et, du sein de la terre, une voix formidable
> Répond en gémissant à ce cri redoutable.   (V.vi.1507,1509)

(A ghastly cry from out of the waters' depths, and from the bowels of the earth a fearsome voice groaned in answer to that terrible cry.)

The sound is that of living beings, frightening or anguished, inhabiting water and earth, powers at work in nature. These eerie sounds are absent from Seneca, who instead describes a storm, while in Euripides the rumble of sound is that of something natural rather than of something uncanny. Racine's account creates a sense of foreboding.

All three dramatists convey the terrifying hugeness of the wave and of the monster which it brings in its wake. Here as elsewhere Racine condenses Seneca's elaborations, while borrowing from him:

> Son front large est armé de cornes menaçantes;
> Tout son corps est couvert d'écailles jaunissantes;
> Indomptable taureau, dragon impétueux,
> Sa croupe se recourbe en replis tortueux.   (V.vi.1517)

(His huge forehead is armed with fearsome horns and his whole body clothed in yellow scales, a formidable bull, a furious dragon, his hindquarters curved in twisting folds.)

Following Seneca, Racine presents Hippolyte's encounter with the monster as single combat, his companions taking refuge. Théramène remarks with faint irony that they refrained from displaying a useless courage (line 1525). In Seneca they are merely petrified with fear. Seneca makes the struggle a set piece with Hippolytus shouting defiance to the bull. The contest goes several 'rounds' and epic (extended) similes are employed. Significantly, Racine is alone in causing his hero to inflict a grievous wound on the monster, after the manner of a dragon-killer of legend, and we remember that Hippolyte's father Thésée was a slayer of monsters. Ironically, in Racine's account, the wounded monster, in its rage and pain:

> leur présente une gueule enflammée
> Qui les couvre de feu, de sang et de fumée   (V.vi.1533)

(turns towards the horses its flaming jaws and covers them with fire, blood and smoke)

startling the horses into flight and out of Hippolyte's control, so that he is dashed on the rocks when his chariot capsizes. Racine, alone of the three dramatists, remarks that a god was said to have been seen goading the horses' dusty flanks (lines 1539–40). And while it is customary to point out that Racine is careful to present the intervention of the god only as hearsay, it must also be noted that he goes out of his way to suggest to the reader that the disaster was perhaps contrived by a supernatural agency.

The dying Hippolyte's protestation of his innocence of crime echoes that in Euripides, and the 'récit de Théramène' nears its close with Hippolyte's recommendation of Aricie to Thésée, necessarily absent from the Greek and Roman versions of the legend. Théramène's last lines evoke with great delicacy Hippolyte's appalling injuries, so graphically described by Seneca.

> ce héros expiré
> N'a laissé dans mes bras qu'un corps défiguré,
> Triste objet, où des dieux triomphe la colére,
> Et que méconnaîtrait l'œil même de son père.   (V.vi.1567)

(the dead hero left in my arms only a disfigured corpse, a grim token of the anger of the gods, that even his father would hardly recognise.)

Naturally, the long moral debate between the dying Hippolytus, Theseus, and Artemis which concludes Euripides' play has barely an echo in Racine's, not merely on the grounds of implausibility, but because his play finds its conclusion in the death of the heroine, which in Euripides has preceded that of Hippolytus.

Contemporary and subsequent criticism of the 'récit de Théramène' was made on the grounds of excessive embellishment, but the *Dissertation sur les tragédies de 'Phèdre et Hippolyte'* (1677) (those of Racine and of his rival Pradon), attributed to Adrien-Thomas Perdou de Subligny, an old enemy of Racine's, raises a familiar objection to the undignified language used by Racine of his noble hero. A certain simplicity in Racine's writing, perhaps owing something to Euripides, is for the modern reader or audience an attraction: as in Euripides, it involves us more closely with the character depicted. Subligny, however, was a follower of Corneille, whose tragedies strive constantly after the elevated and the imposing.

Subligny asks whether it is acceptable to speak of a Prince feeding his horses with his own hands (line 1548), or of a god goading their dusty flanks (line 1540). He observes scornfully that he cannot bear Racine's making a god a drover and a Prince a groom. But, clearly, the allusion to Hippolyte's feeding his own horses emphasises the close relationship which he has with them, a recurrent motif of the play. Subligny's allusion to the divine goadsman or drover is more plausible. But we must think not of a drover but of Neptune with his trident. More important is the fact that the allusion to a god is made. Subligny speaks also of the unlikelihood that a messenger announcing to a father the death of his son should devote himself to describing the fine horses which killed him, the curls of their manes and their harness. Nor would he represent them lowering their heads and ears in shame like hacks. It would be quite unnatural for a father to listen patiently to these useless descriptions. Subligny is insensitive to the misfortune of these fine creatures.

Some of the descriptive embellishments which critics were to object to derive from the ornate Seneca. Fénelon deplores the pompous and florid description of the form of the dragon (*Lettre à l'Académie* (1714), Ch. VI). Voltaire admits to not caring overmuch for the dragon's 'yellowish scales' (*Questions sur l'Encyclopédie* (1770), art. 'Amplification'). This fabulous beast obviously captured Racine's imagination and, like Seneca, he makes his monster evil, loathsome, and uncanny. But certainly he has learnt Euripides' lesson of economy and relevance. To some extent, reactions here will be subjective. Readers or audience will be more, or less, tolerant of the inclusion of descriptive detail in speeches of tragic import.

Voltaire, at all events, offers a cogent reply to criticisms that Théramène needed to say only that 'Your son's no more [...] I have seen the best of mortals die' (lines 1492–3), observing that Thésée himself asks to be told how it happened: 'Quel coup me l'a ravi? quelle foudre soudaine?' (line 1497; What blow, what sudden thunderbolt snatched him from me?). It is surely natural that Thésée should wish to know how his son died. Moreover, Théramène is no ordinary messenger, but is Hippolyte's tutor and guardian. It is after all not obvious, given Racine's plot, that it would have sufficed, as Fénelon claimed, for Théramène to say simply that Hippolyte was dead and that he saw him killed by a monster from the sea sent by the gods. For although this might well have been sufficient to introduce a scene of grief and anguished reflection on Thésée's part, more is needed, a more elaborate prelude is required for the tragic finale of which Phèdre herself forms the centre. After the tension, activity, and excitement of the narrative of Hippolyte's death comes the awesome and ominous calm of Phèdre's farewell.

Phèdre was not present when Théramène gave his account of Hippolyte's death, and it has been said that the 'récit' is addressed much less to Thésée than to the spectator, who is attending a ritual which must be respected (Maulnier, *Lecture de Phèdre*, p.108). This interpretation is perhaps a little metaphysical, but the sense of the appalling catastrophe which has resulted from Phèdre's passion for Hippolyte hangs ominously and crushingly over the final scenes and over Phèdre herself. She whom Théramène calls Hippolyte's 'mortal enemy', and whom Thésée describes bitterly as triumphing over her victim, advances slowly to hear Thésée's anguished expression of his resolve to flee the scene of his son's death and the atmosphere of suspicion surrounding his relationship with Phèdre. Thésée prefers to remain ignorant rather than to learn unbearable truths. Like Aricie, whose grief is reported by Théramène (lines 1583–6), Thésée reflects bitterly on the ways of the gods

and the grim irony of their response to his call for punishment
of Hippolyte:

> Je hais jusques aux soins dont m'honorent les dieux,
> Et je m'en vais pleurer leurs faveurs meurtrières,
> Sans plus les fatiguer d'inutiles prières.
> Quoi qu'ils fissent pour moi, leur funeste bonté
> Ne me saurait payer de ce qu'ils m'ont ôté.   (V.vi.1612)

(I hate even the attentions with which the gods honour me, and now I
must lament their murderous favours, no longer tiring them with
useless prayers. For all they have done for me, their fatal aid cannot
make up for what they have robbed me of.)

But Phèdre is resolved to tell the truth and restore the purity of
a daylight which has been sullied by her criminal passion.
While this is clearly expressive of a need to quiet her conscience, the formulation is suggestive of an ancient pagan
purification rite, with Phèdre the sacrificial victim.

Phèdre's dying speech is brief, contrasting markedly with
that of Euripides' Hippolytus. If it is penitent and expiatory, it
nonetheless displays a readiness to shift blame on to the
shoulders of Œnone (lines 1625–26). Œnone herself had earlier
described her rejection by Phèdre as 'well deserved'. But if
Racine is concerned to make us see Phèdre as involuntarily
criminal, her crime pollutes nevertheless. Phèdre has a need to
confess that it was she who lusted after Hippolyte and not he
after her. Were it not for this need to declare Hippolyte's
innocence, she would (she makes it clear) already have put
herself to the sword, but she has chosen a slower death by
poison in order to have time to make her confession:

> J'ai voulu, devant vous exposant mes remords,
> Par un chemin plus lent descendre chez les morts.
>
> (V.vii.1635)

(I wished, confessing my remorse to you, to take a slower path down
to the dead.)

The choice is theatrical; the periphrasis, 'Par un chemin plus
lent descendre chez les morts', is chillingly sinister. The verses
convey an awesome sense of calm acceptance of annihilation.
Phèdre's consciousness fades, and with it her role on life's

stage. Purity is restored to the light of day, and it is as if
Phèdre had never been.

The conventional banality of the lady-in-waiting's 'She dies,
my lord', is followed by a concluding speech of Thésée's which
some have also found banal in its conventionality:

> D'une action si noire
> Que ne peut avec elle expirer la mémoire!
> Allons, de mon erreur, hélas! trop éclaircis,
> Mêler nos pleurs au sang de mon malheureux fils!
>
> Rendons-lui les honneurs qu'il a trop mérités,
> Et, pour mieux apaiser ses mânes irrités,
> Que malgré les complots d'une injuste famille
> Son amante aujourd'hui me tienne lieu de fille!
>
> (V.vii.1645, 1651)

(Would that the memory of her appalling crime could die with her!
Let us, now that my error is all too clear, mingle our tears with the
blood of my unhappy son! Let us render him the honours he has so
well deserved and the better to appease the anger of his shade let his
beloved, despite the plotting of an unjust family, be as a daughter to
me from this day!)

If this conclusion could be seen as illustrating the Racinian
conception of tragic catharsis, whereby the audience's
emotions of pity and fear are reduced to a state of moderation
and conformity to reason, it cannot be said to express the
tragic sense of the play. Thésée seeks to forget, to close a
chapter, to reconcile. The ideals of justice and honour remain,
but rather as objects of piety than as forces which shape and
give meaning to existence.

Meaning

The tragedy of *Phèdre* is a tale of illicit passion, jealousy, false
witness, the death of an innocent victim, and the despairing
suicides of two culprits. In his Preface to the play, however,
Racine shows himself anxious to defend its edifying character.
He claims never to have written a play in which virtue is more
in evidence: 'The mere thought of crime is regarded in it with
as much horror as the crime itself. Amorous failings are

regarded as true failings: the passions are displayed there only to reveal all the excesses of which they are the cause, and vice is depicted everywhere in the play in colours which make its ugliness recognisable and hateful.' Yet in the first paragraph of the Preface Racine is concerned to find extenuating circumstances for Phèdre's illicit desires.

It may seem puzzling to find Racine saying of Euripides: 'if I owed to him only the idea of Phèdre, I could say that I owe to him the most reasonable thing that I have put on the stage.' But Euripides' Phaedra is motivated by a concern to preserve her reputation and not to admit to being at the mercy of an irrational desire. Similarly, Phèdre, according to Racine, is the first to feel horror at her illicit passion: 'She makes every effort to overcome it. She prefers to allow herself to die rather than to confess it to anyone, and when she is forced to reveal it, she speaks of it with a shame which makes it very obvious that her crime is rather a punishment by the gods than a movement of her will.' But the notion of crime as punishment is distinctly odd. There seem to be two moral codes in operation here: what is punishment for the one, that of Venus, being crime for the other – say, that of Minos, Phèdre's father. It is clear that Racine's own moral judgement coincides with that which condemns as criminal the desires which have been inflicted on Phèdre as a punishment. Racine's moral code is the code of Minos and of Phèdre herself.

It remains a question why Racine is so concerned to make Phèdre appear as innocent as possible. The analogous concern of Euripides is much more readily intelligible. He seeks to show the cruelty, the irrationality, the contradictoriness of the gods, or of the forces that work upon human beings, and the tragedy which results. Phèdre stands out as a particularly powerful example of a type of character seen in several of Racine's plays, a character tortured by the reproaches of conscience. Only in Phèdre, however, do we find what can be called a sense of sin, which arises from the felt incestuousness or unnatural character of her desires. Nevertheless, to interpret *Phèdre* as a Christian, perhaps a Jansenist, play as is sometimes done, raises difficulties. Voltaire recounts that, in his childhood (in the early years of the eighteenth century), he often heard applied to Phèdre the Jansenist formula 'a just (wo)man in whom the grace of God was lacking' (Letter of 23 December 1760, D9492). But the lines spoken by Œnone to Phèdre, which are cited in evidence:

> Vous aimez. On ne peut vaincre sa destinée.
> Par un charme fatal vous fûtes entraînée   (IV.vi.1297)

(You are in love. We cannot change our destiny. You were carried away by a fateful spell)

express an unqualified fatalism and magical beliefs which are totally un-Christian. Understanding of Jansenist theology had become profoundly corrupted. Equally, to speak of Phèdre as a 'reprobate Christian', as Racine's great Jansenist contemporary, Antoine Arnauld, was alleged to have done, and as Chateaubriand was to do a century later (in *Le Génie du christianisme* (1802), II, iii, 3), is to ignore the ostensible and, in large measure, actual paganism of the content and ethos of the play. For the Christian there is a single omnipotent deity and all is under his providence, whereas in the world of Racine's play, there is a plurality of independent deities with conflicting aims and policies which produce moral anarchy and disaster. As with Euripides, we are back with the gods of Homer.

Racine can, of course, have had no belief in the pagan gods whom he depicts, and it has been argued analogously that Euripides, a sophisticated thinker, could have had no belief in the mythological figures that he represented in his plays. In both cases it is asserted that in consequence the plays are to be interpreted as psychological drama, the gods being symbolic of human drives and passions. Nevertheless, in both the *Hippolytus* of Euripides and the *Phèdre* of Racine, the gods are deliberately given prominence. Euripides appears actually to have introduced the roles of Aphrodite and Artemis into his play, these having been absent from the first version (now lost). Racine's *Phèdre* is filled with allusions to the gods as no other of his plays hitherto had been. Both works give a patently religious account of the human predicament but without espousing any definable religious doctrine.

It is of interest for any conjectured religious interpretation of Racine's play that the equivocal Artemis is replaced by Minos as an authoritative source of value judgement, the remote source being the sun-god. Whereas in Euripides two goddesses, Aphrodite and Artemis, compete for the allegiance of mortals, in the shadowy presence of the great god Zeus, himself no better than he should be, Racine's Phèdre, 'the daughter of Minos and Pasiphaë', is torn between conscience and passion, each as relentless as the other. Whereas Pascal wrote of the wretchedness of man without God, the sheer mercilessness of the way of things in Racine's play is such that one is tempted to see it as revealing rather the wretchedness of man *with* God, driven as Phèdre is by a harrowing conscience of Baudelairean malignity.

As Racine observes in his Preface, Phèdre did not choose to lust after Hippolyte. Her passion was inflicted on her by a goddess. Yet she has an intense sense of guilt. For her passion has sullied her, made her feel unclean. Only death, annihilation, can remove the tarnish from the light of day. By her suicide, Phèdre in a sense displays her freedom to choose her fate. In another sense, she accomplishes her destiny: to be destroyed by the passion which consumes her. The tragic action is both human and divine: human beings may act freely; they cannot free themselves from divine causality. This conception, both pagan and Christian, conflicts with ordinary logic, and may seem tolerable only if one can believe that there is an overarching just order of things. Neither the *Hippolytus* of Euripides nor Racine's *Phèdre* affords us that solace. 'What can the gods do for men, except destroy them?' a scholar asks at the end of a discussion of causation in the *Hippolytus*, and adds: 'Human beings can at least forgive one another, even if the gods cannot forgive' (Winnington-Ingram, 'Hippolytus: A Study in Causation', *Entretiens sur l'antiquité classique*, VI, *Euripide*, Geneva, 1958, p.191). But, in Racine's play, Hippolyte must die before he is forgiven (although he appears to forgive his father). And certainly there is no forgiveness for Phèdre. Only Thésée and Aricie are drawn together by their loss, to make what they can of a shattered world.

The play is not easily interpreted in simple human terms, for the heroine cannot be treated as a free agent living her life in accord with her own desires and will. If the gods are to be taken as symbolic of forces at work within human beings, then those forces must be seen as alien, as forces which possess and obsess, not as part of an integrated personality. Phèdre herself is not merely torn between passion and conscience, but harassed by them. Her faculty of moral judgement has become a destructive sense of guilt which seems as pathological as the passion which is its object. It is the aura of irrationality and perverted value-judgement – illicit desire interpreted as punishment, conscience grown neurotic – which confers a sense of hopeless anguish on the play. That, however, was plainly not how Racine wished us to see it.

Chapter 3

The posterity of *Phèdre*

Racine's *Phèdre* was the object of a conspiracy to bring about its failure. He had his enemies among the admirers of Corneille and those who championed the Moderns against the Ancients, or classicising writers. Cornelians and Moderns were often the same people. Moreover, Racine's rapid rise to fame was too striking for him not to make a number of enemies among other writers and their protectors. He had already had, with *Iphigénie* (1674), the experience of rival authors planning to put on a play on the same subject as his own in the hope of outdoing it, and he had had no hesitation in taking measures to have the performance of the rival play deferred. Similarly, the dramatist Jacques (also known as Nicolas) Pradon, an admirer of Corneille, was put up to composing a play entitled *Phèdre et Hippolyte* (modern edition by O. Classe, Exeter, 1987) in competition with Racine's. Pradon had a grievance against Racine, believing that Racine had been instrumental in getting his own play *Tamerlan* (1675) taken off when running very successfully. Legend has it that boxes were bought up for the performances of Racine's and Pradon's plays on the subject of Phèdre and Hippolyte, so that the one play should be performed to empty seats and the other to a large audience. It appears that this was not so, but Pradon's play, which, like other French plays on the same theme, shrinks from making Phèdre the wife of Thésée, seems to have been sufficiently successful for a while to cause Racine some anxiety. Pradon's success, however, lasted only a matter of weeks, while Racine's play has never ceased to be regarded as one of the great masterpieces of world literature.

The great brilliance of the achievement of the tragedians Corneille and Racine posed well-nigh insoluble problems for their successors. Only dramatists of equal genius could have successfully followed the French classical example, and they were lacking. The plays of Corneille and Racine offered models, techniques, forms, which were regularly imitated, but such imitations lacked the imaginative vitality of their models. It was not till the second half of the eighteenth century that fair success was achieved in efforts to renew tragedy by escaping from the classical mould.

In Restoration England attempts had been made to introduce the public to the French classical dramatists in translation. Some success was had with Corneille, but Racine had on the whole to wait for the eighteenth century. One thinks of Ambrose Philips' adaptation of *Andromaque* under the title *The Distrest Mother* (1712) and Sir Roger de Coverly's description of Hermione as 'a notable young baggage'. *Phèdre*, however, fell into the hands of the minor poet and dramatist Edmund (Neale) Smith (1670–1742). His *Phaedra and Hippolitus* appeared in 1707. The *dramatis personae* are Theseus, Hippolitus, Lycon, Minister of State (who appears to be Phèdre's confidant), Cratander, captain of the guards, Phaedra, and Ismena, a captive Princess in love with Hippolitus (taking the role of Racine's Aricie but bearing the name of that character's confidant). Racine's play is indeed much adapted, and the tone, supposing that one can speak of a single tone, is very uncertain. The neo-classicising theatre of the end of the seventeenth century in England still affected the ranting rhetoric of earlier heroic tragedy and was totally out of tune with Racinian dignity and rhythmic delicacy.

The plot is certainly largely indebted to Racine's, with sundry accretions – or excrescences. Theseus is pronounced dead and then returns, upsetting the plans of Phaedra and Lycon. Lycon is something of the villain of the piece with designs of his own and is denounced both by Phaedra (twice) and by Theseus. The role of Ismena/Aricie is developed. She professes her willingness to die and let Hippolitus marry Phaedra if that means he will be safe. She is jealous of Phaedra rather than the reverse. There are possible reminiscences here of Racine's heroine Atalide in *Bajazet*, as there are of the crafty Acomat of that play in Lycon's advice to Phaedra to feign love for Theseus, and perhaps in his cunning designs. The confession scene between Phaedra and Hippolitus with the incriminating evidence provided by the sword, and the scenes between Theseus and Hippolytus, follow Racine – at some distance. Cratander fills the role of the messenger, announcing tersely that Hippolitus has committed suicide by his sword.

The flavour of the play can be sufficiently indicated with a couple of speeches of Phaedra's. She declaims her self-loathing for allowing Hippolitus to be falsely denounced:

> Now, *Minos*, I defy thee;
> Ev'n all thy dreadful Magazines of Pains,
> Stones, Furies, Wheels are slight to what I suffer,
> And Hell it self's relief.

So much for Phèdre's agonised conscience. And in the last act she apostrophises the dead Hippolitus with a conceit:

> Thee I pursue, (Oh great ill-fated Youth!)
> Pursue thee still, but now with chast Desires;
> Thee thro' the dismal waste of gloomy Death;
> Thee thro' the glimmering Dawn, and purer Day,
> Thro' all the Elysian Plains: O righteous *Minos*!
> *Elysian* Plains! There he and his *Ismena*
> Shall sport for ever, shall for ever drink
> Immortal Love; while all the blackest ghosts
> Shrink from the baleful sight of one more monstrous
> And more accurst than they.

The jealousy which in Racine impelled Phèdre to take the fatal step of acquiescence in the false accusation against Hippolyte, for which she finally atones in death, here becomes a scene of imagined anguish after death. Finally, Phaedra sacrifices herself not to her conscience but to her desire for Hippolitus.

Phaedra having stabbed herself to death, Hippolitus unexpectedly turns up again to explain that he had only pretended to stab himself and had then made his escape. The joy of Theseus, Ismena, and Hippolitus is but slightly tempered by thoughts of Phaedra's pathetic death. The play ends by offering a double measure of the reassuring platitudes with which tragedies commonly ended:

THESEUS
Then learn from me, ye Kings that rule the World,
With equal poize, let steddy Justice sway,
And flagrant Crimes with certain Vengeance pay,
But till the proofs are clear the Stroak delay.
HIPPOLITUS
The righteous Gods that innocence require,
Protect the Goodness which themselves inspire;
Unguarded Vertue Human Arts defies,
Th'Accus'd is happy, while th'Accuser dies.

Respectable citizens could evidently sleep safely in their beds.

The amateur of French classical drama will enjoy this remarkable farrago of moral, psychological, dramatic, and rhetorical pomposity for its unconscious humour. It seems that the play was not at first very successful, and may well have been found bewildering. It apparently had more success in the 1720s and later. It is to be hoped that this was not because the audience supposed itself to be acquiring a deeper insight into Racinian tragedy. In Dublin, in 1759, the Irish-English composer Thomas Roseingrave (1690–1766) had great success with his opera *Phaedra and Hippolitus*, of which the libretto was based on Edmund Smith's play. A good deal of rewriting must have been necessary to impart to the work the necessary lyrical quality.

If we are looking for echoes of the true voice of Racinian tragedy, we shall have to turn, however paradoxically, to the Abbé Prévost's novel entitled *Histoire du Chevalier Des Grieux et de Manon Lescaut* (first edition 1731), better known under the simple but misleading title *Manon Lescaut*, for Des Grieux is the central figure and it is he who is to be compared to Phèdre. In describing his irresistible passion for Manon, the former seminarist Des Grieux is prone to using the language of theology but as Raymond Picard, editor of Racine and of *Manon Lescaut*, has noted, Des Grieux's account of his plight belongs to a literary rather than a theological tradition. He uses the language of tragedy in describing himself as a hapless victim of fate, and if, like Phèdre, he considers his passion shameful, he nevertheless persists in it (*Manon Lescaut*, ed. R. Picard (Paris 1965), pp. cxxx, cxxxii). As some have done for Phèdre, Des Grieux draws an analogy between his 'irresistible' passion and the Jansenist conception of man's enslavement to sin, illustrating yet again the corruption which Jansenist theology had suffered through vulgarisation. But he is equally prone to employ very un-Jansenistic casuistical arguments in self-justification, claiming for himself an essential goodness of heart unaffected by his squalid behaviour. Of such casuistry in Phèdre, whose self-condemnation is continual, there is nevertheless a hint. Both Phèdre and Des Grieux appeal to the sensibility of the reader – and Racine's plays appealed particularly in that way to eighteenth-century audiences – but Phèdre is not the fully-fledged (wo)man of sensibility that Des Grieux is. On the other hand, *Manon Lescaut* preserves a tragic sense of the tension between fate, responsibility, and conscience comparable with that of *Phèdre*, and rare in the literature of the French Enlightenment. One has to look to the anguished *Candide* (1759) of Prévost's longer-lived contemporary, Voltaire, for a sense of tragedy of equal or greater power. Prévost's and Voltaire's metaphysical anguish has its roots in the seventeenth century.

If the immense achievements and prestige of seventeenth-century French tragedy constituted an intimidating challenge to imitators, opera had become increasingly popular from the later years of the seventeenth century onwards and the designation 'tragédie lyrique' or 'tragédie en musique' indicates its close links with the theatre proper. Opera, in contrast with neo-classical tragedy, made a strong appeal to the senses, and audiences were attracted by spectacle and scenic effect. This lavish and costly entertainment, with its commonly mythological and legendary plots featuring heroic characters, expressed an aristocratic ethos and prolonged its life into a century, and certainly into a literature, which was becoming increasingly influenced by the outlook and tastes of the bourgeoisie.

The greatest operatic composer of eighteenth-century France, and perhaps France's greatest musician, was Jean-Philippe Rameau (1683–1764). He was fortunate in the choice of librettist for his first operatic masterpiece, *Hippolyte et*

Aricie of 1733. Abbé Simon-Joseph Pellegrin (1663–1745) was one of the best two or three librettists of the first half of the eighteenth century in France. Having written several books of religious poetry – to popular tunes – and some tragedies, he wrote the libretto to *Médée et Jason* (1713) and was to compose the libretti for eight other operas. *Hippolyte et Aricie* (1733) was the last of these. Pellegrin was seventy years of age, Rameau fifty and at the beginning of his operatic career.

Pellegrin makes his excuses in his preface for following in the footsteps of Racine. The characters are those of Racine except that the messenger is now named Arcas, and that the gods and goddesses have roles in the play, and there are priestesses, citizens of Troezen, huntsmen and shepherds. He makes the secondary plot of Aricie and Hippolyte into the main one. The love between Hippolyte and Aricie, Phèdre's jealousy, and the explanation of Thésée's absence are taken from Racine. The abduction of Hippolyte by Diana comes from Ovid. Pellegrin follows Virgil or some other ancient author or an allusion in Racine's Preface to *Phèdre* in marrying Hippolyte to Aricie. A contemporary illustration shows Hippolyte seated on a throne, surrounded by putti, looking very pleased with himself, Aricie on one side and Diana on the other. While some see Hippolyte and Aricie as having the main roles, others nevertheless claim that it is the tragic figures of Thésée and Phèdre who dominate the drama. And certainly Phèdre has some moving passages. Some of the most exquisite of Rameau's music is evoked by her prayer to Venus (III.i) and her expression of remorse at Hippolyte's death (IV.iv). But Thésée is the most tragic figure in the opera, and the scenes of Act V in which he laments the loss of his son are particularly moving:

THÉSÉE

Grands Dieux! de quels remords je me sens déchiré!
Que d'horreurs à la fois! J'ai vu Phèdre expirer.
Quel mystère odieux! Quel amour détestable
La perfide, en mourant, vient de me déclarer!
Mon fils ... O douleur qui m'accable!
Il était innocent. Dieux, que je suis coupable!
Rentrons dans les enfers! qui peut me retenir!

D'un monstre tel que moi délivrons la nature!
De la plus horrible imposture
Les perfides auteurs viennent de se punir.
Mes parricides vœux ont consommé le crime,
Et je dois à mon fils sa dernière victime.
Dieu des Mers, aux mortels cache-moi pour jamais!
(*Thésée veut se précipiter dans la mer.*)

(O gods! with what remorse I am torn!
So many horrors all at once! I have seen Phaedra die.
What an abominable mystery! What an execrable passion
The traitress has revealed to me in dying!
My son ... O overwhelming grief!
He was innocent. O gods, how great is my guilt!
To Hell I must return! Who shall prevent me!
Let nature be rid of a monster such as I!
For this most horrible deceit
Its perpetrators have punished themselves.
My parricidal oaths have crowned the crime,
And I owe my son its last victim.
God of the Seas, hide me forever from mortal sight!
(*Theseus makes to throw himself into the sea.*))

Both Hippolyte and Thésée are in fact saved, but Thésée is condemned to the anguish of eternal separation from his son, who is reunited with Aricie in her grove in Italy.

Given that Rameau was to be the object of attack in mid century by the French apostles of the Italian opera buffa or light opera, it is notable that the gifted Italian composer Tommaso Traetta (1727–79) created an opera entitled *Ippolito ed Aricia* (1759) to a libretto translated from that of Pellegrin by Carlo Innocenzio Frugoni. It appears that Traetta's aim was to take over the traditional structure of French opera which, with its emphasis upon declamation, spectacle, ballet, and chorus, in fact retained many of the features of traditional Italian opera which, for its part, had developed a concern rather with bel canto. Significantly, Frugoni found Pellegrin's libretto inadequate and went back to Racine's text in search of material for fine arias. It does not appear, however, that the dramatic power of the opera benefited from these additions. Nevertheless, one can see in Frugoni's and Traetta's return to Racine evidence of the lyrical power of his poetry, even where he had not been writing with a musical setting in view (see Daniel Heartz, 'Operatic Reform at Parma. *Ippolito ed Aricia'*, *Atti del convegno sul settecento Parmense* (Parma, 1969), p. 272).

Another operatic version of *Phèdre* was created in 1786 by the able French librettist F. B. Hoffman (1760–1828). His libretto was set to music by J. B. Lemoyne (1751–96), who claimed to be a pupil of Gluck. Aricie does not appear, and Hoffman abstains from pillaging Racine's own verses – out of respect for Racine so he says. He may possibly not have approved of the introduction of a romantic interest into the ancient tragic tale. His characters are Phèdre, Hippolyte, Thésée, Œnone, and the regulation huntsmen, ladies-in-waiting, and priestesses – this time of Venus. The relationships and reactions of the main characters are similar to those in Racine and it is the nurse who denounces Hippolyte to Thésée, but her relationship with Phèdre is not so close or significant. The writing is somewhat conventional and platitudinous, though it could well have succeeded lyrically.

A good sample of the libretto, echoing some of the most famous verses of Racine's play, is the following monologue of Phèdre:

> Je souille l'air que je respire,
> Mon aspect inspire l'horreur,
> Un affreux remords me déchire,
> Toi qui vois à tes pieds ta fille criminelle,
> Soleil, dont je ternis l'éclat majestueux,
> Obscurcis-toi, ta splendeur immortelle
> Ne doit plus briller à mes yeux.

> (I pollute the air that I breathe,
> My sight inspires horror,
> A fearful remorse rends me.
> You who see at your feet your criminal daughter,
> O Sun, whose majestic brilliancy I tarnish,
> Grow dim, your immortal splendour
> Must no longer shine before my eyes.)

Hoffman recasts Racine's bold image of the brightness of day sullied by Phèdre's eyes, and turns it into something logical and prosaic.

The play offers no real explanation of Phèdre's conscientious doubts and anguish – and like Thésée she is inclined to repeat herself: several times declaring herself about to die. But this may be for the benefit of the composer in need of lyrical material. Hoffman refused to include this play in his collected works. No doubt he considered it too glaringly inferior to Racine's tragedy, although as a libretto it has merits.

Two verse translations of *Phèdre* have come down to us from the end of the eighteenth century or the beginning of the nineteenth. One is in Spanish and the other in German. The Spanish translation, published in Barcelona, is anonymous and undated. It was a century in which attempts were made to acclimatise French classical drama in Spain, although these encountered resistance from national tradition. The translation is close and accurate, its only peculiarity being that it concludes with the lines (of Theseus):

> Would that the memory
> Of her appalling crime might die with her!

– a moral ending omitting Racine's last eight lines which offer reconciliation with Aricie. This may reflect the moralising view of the aims of literature prevalent in some quarters in eighteenth-century Spain. On the other hand, Thésée's last speech had long been considered to be too flat after the anguish of what precedes.

The German translation, dating from 1804 5, has much more obvious significance, if only in virtue of the distinction of the translator, who was none other than Friedrich Schiller (1759–1805). It is a remarkable translation into unrhymed iambic pentameters, often line by line, but showing little sign of strain or awkwardness, although the loss of two syllables from each line in comparison with the French alexandrine entails some reduction of content – and a tendency to eliminate the use of periphrastic description so frequent in Racine. One should not overlook, however, Racine's own use from time to time of repetition ('J'ai vu, Seigneur, j'ai vu . . .', etc.) to fill out his alexandrines. Schiller's translation into German displays precision and ease, and imitates very successfully the flexible rhythms of the French, an essential quality of Racinian verse. Schiller achieves this to a considerable extent by a free use of enjambment, supposedly forbidden by classical rules but not absent from Racine's own verse or alien to it.

It is not easy to determine what significance to attach to Schiller's choice of *Phèdre* for translation, apart from the high esteem in which French tragedy was held at Weimar and the particular fame of Racine's *Phèdre*. Schiller, who had been seriously ill, said that he undertook the translation at the end of 1804 because he did not yet feel up to creative work of his own and did not wish to be idle. He began his translation of this 'Paradepferd' (showpiece) of the French stage on 17 December and completed it in twenty-six days. It was then performed at court.

Schiller certainly strove to imitate the style and structure of the French classical theatre, and the close attention to the detail of a great French classical play which the translation of *Phèdre* entailed undoubtedly contributed to, or revealed, his mastery of classical form. It seems doubtful, on the other hand, whether Schiller's own classical plays have a truly Racinian ring. Admittedly, it has been pointed out that in his own work 'Schiller created heroes who acquire involuntary guilt, being blinded by passion and circumstance which overwhelm them'. And it has been contended that Schiller's great tragedies reveal the same pessimistic outlook as Racine's *Phèdre*. 'Phèdre in dying, however, regains her royal bearing. In assenting to her fate and atoning for her misdeed she retrieves her dignity as a human being' (Peter André Bloch, *Schiller und die französische klassische Tragödie* (Düsseldorf 1968) pp. 315, 260–1). But this gives a much more positive value to Phèdre's death than Racine's play suggests, with its sense of hopelessness, emptiness, and futility. Like the more or less contemporary *Suréna* of Corneille (his last play) or *La Princesse de Clèves* of Madame de Lafayette, Racine's *Phèdre* raises the question whether human aspiration after an ideal has any significance. There is a fin-de-siècle air about such works, a sense that an old order is disintegrating. The forceful Schiller resembles rather a pessimistic version of the idealistic early

Corneille. But for Corneille, guilt is a forensic rather than a metaphysical concept and one can see why the great German tragedian, preoccupied with the problem of the relation between fate, freedom, and responsibility, should be attracted by Racine's *Phèdre*, in which that problem takes on an agonising intensity.

With the Romantic period, as the adjective implies, we leave behind the essentially classical character of the *Phèdre* legend – the sense of an immutable moral order and of the corruption which accompanies offence against it. A Romantic echo of *Phèdre* is heard in the *René* of Chateaubriand (1768–1848) who, in a Preface of 1805, observes that he would have chosen the subject of *Phèdre* had it not already been treated by Racine. *René* is the story of the incestuous passion of the young eponymous hero for his sister Amélie, who pines away for love of him, takes refuge in religious vows, and eventually commits suicide. Chateaubriand emphasises the theme of incest, the physical effects of passion, the horror of suicide, and their conflict with the precepts of religion. The austere inner conflict of Phèdre with its metaphysical anguish is transformed into an emotional indulgence followed by some stern moralising. Chateaubriand succeeds in doing exactly what seventeenth-century moralists declaimed against, and what *Phèdre* does not do or attempt to do, namely to make illicit passion alluring. The analogies between *René* and *Phèdre* are really rather slight.

Closer to Racine's *Phèdre* is Emile Zola's novel *La Curée* of 1872, which he conceived of as a 'new *Phèdre*'. The young heroine, Renée, married to an older man, a financial speculator, develops a voluptuous passion for Maxime, his young, effeminate, and cynical son by a previous marriage. As with Racine's *Phèdre*, the relationship is not of blood relatives, but the impression given of its highly sinful character adds spice to it. Zola titillates the reader with his sex scenes. There is a kind of glamour for Renée in the illicit relationship which is absent from Racine. She nevertheless feels remorse, so that her state of mind has something of the 'conscience dans le mal' of Baudelaire, but without its religious overtones. The analogy between her own situation and Phèdre's is brought home to her when present at a performance of Racine's play – her whole attention being absorbed by the state of mind of the actress in the central role. The reactions of her lover Maxime are more frivolous. When he is married off to a young lady with a large dowry, Renée remembers her *Phèdre* and takes revenge by denouncing him to her husband as having seduced her. A sardonic twist (the most original aspect of the relationship) is given to the tale by the decision of her old and faithful servant Céleste (counterpart of Phèdre's Œnone) – who now seems to her all she has left – to leave her service, having amassed the five thousand francs that she had worked to acquire in order to retire. Father and son meanwhile are seen hobnobbing amicably together. Renée dies untragically of meningitis. The cynicism or amorality of the tale precludes the possibility of a tragic meaning, which would require tense conflict between impulse and a moral imperative. The positive evaluation of rebellion against order, which characterises a Romantic ethos, militates against the classical quest for a theodicy or secularised equivalent.

A moral could be more readily found in the drawing-room drama *Renée*, derived largely from *La Curée* at the behest of Sarah Bernhardt who, like several theatre directors, was shocked by what Zola finally wrote, so that the play had to wait several years before it was produced in 1887. This tale of a marriage of convenience between an adventurer with mercenary ambitions and an heiress of damaged reputation, her act of adultery with her stepson in a moment of weakness, and her suicide by shooting when her suddenly amorous and jealous husband intervenes, has not much to do with fate or hereditary defect of character, more with social evils and the corrupting role of money. Zola compares the sober complexion of his play to that of Racine's *Phèdre*, but the sobriety of *Renée* reflects the conventional bourgeois milieu in which it is set and is quite unlike the austere grandeur of Racine's *Phèdre*.

The verse drama *Fedra* (1909) of Gabriele D'Annunzio (1863–1938) must itself be accounted Romantic (if not decadent). It is, however, vastly different from Zola's works on the theme. D'Annunzio's play is ambitiously mythological, with a cast and settings suitable for a spectacular opera. It furnished, indeed, the libretto for the opera *Fedra* (1915) of Pizzetti. The *personae fabulae* comprise Fedra, Ippolito, Teseo, the Æther, the messenger, the bard, Gorgo the nurse, the Theban slave (whom Fedra intends to marry off to Ippolito), the Phoenician pirate, suppliants, youths, foot soldiers, charioteers, riders and huntsmen. And the printed text offers a pretentious *Rerum Insignium Index* (Index of Noteworthy Features) including such things as the zither of Daedalus, the dance of Helen, the bow of Artemis, most of which have nothing to do with Fedra. The play is indeed largely evocative and descriptive, and luxuriantly rhetorical.

Little happens until two-thirds of the way through the play, when Fedra reveals her love to Ippolito with a passionate kiss, which he says is not that of a mother. There are one or two perverse echoes of Racinian phraseology. Ippolito calls Fedra 'figlia di Pasifae' (D'Annunzio has no truck with Minos) and Fedra apostrophises the light of day: 'O Luce, che per l'ultima volta ora ti vegga! (O Light, may I now see you for the last time!). It is Fedra herself who accuses Ippolito of assault and he is duly destroyed by Nettuno at Teseo's request. An interesting touch is that Fedra is made the inaugurator of the legendary cult of Hippolytus among young brides-to-be.

The outcome of the play is quite contrary to that of its classical predecessors. Fedra is a rebel. When Teseo accuses her of lying, she throws back at him his own cruel treatment of her sister Antiope. And she defies Artemis:

> Ippolito è meco.
> Velato all'Invisibile
> lo porterò su le mie braccia azzurre,
> perché l'amo. O Purissima, da te
> ei se credette amato, e ti chiamò.
> Ma l'amor d'una dea può esser vile.

> (Hippolytus is with me.
> Veiled from the Invisible
> I will carry him on my azure arms,
> because I love him. O Most Pure, by you
> he thought himself loved, and cried to you.
> But the love of a goddess may be craven.)

In the melodramatic final scene, Fedra, about to expire on the veiled body of Ippolito, smiles up to the heavens:

> Vi sorride
> O stelle, su l'entrare della Notte,
> Fedra indimenticabile!

> (She smiles at you,
> O stars, as Night falls,
> Fedra, the unforgettable!)

But this famous victory of sensuality over chastity is hollow. There has been no battle, only a vast deployment of ego. The pretentious bravado of this essentially fin-de-siècle spectacular sends us back, unenriched, to that earlier not quite fin-de-siècle tragedy in which a still small voice lends Racine's Phèdre her poignant dignity in defeat.

D'Annunzio's is perhaps the last and the most flamboyant of the Romantic Phaedras. Subsequent works have made the legendary heroine the vehicle for a serious exploration of the personal, moral, or social consequences of obsessive sexual desire. Theological, mythological, or metaphysical considerations are losing their power to move. And that may be the lesson to be drawn from D'Annunzio's showpiece.

The Spanish essayist, novelist, and poet, Miguel de Unamuno (1864–1936) presents his prose drama *Fedra* (1910–11) as a Christian tragedy, the basic argument of which he describes vaguely as that of Euripides *or* Racine, while the plot is quite different. There is no indication that the characters are of noble birth. Fedra and Hipólito are retained from legend, and Hipólito is a countryman fond of the hunt. The nurse becomes Eustaquià, Fedra's confidant. Fedra's husband is however called Pedro and has none of the legendary features of Theseus. There is a somewhat free-thinking doctor, Marcelo, and a servant, Rosa, in whose marriage Fedra takes an interest. Fedra confesses her love to Hipólito, and is repulsed. She denounces him to her husband, who orders him to leave. Fedra, a pious Catholic, filled with a sense of guilt and sin, takes an overdose of drugs, leaving a confession for her husband. Pedro and Hipólito, who blames himself for his insensitivity, are reconciled. The play reads like a rhetorically emotional eighteenth-century French bourgeois *drame*. Of its classical and neo-classical sources almost nothing of significance is retained. There are some undeveloped allusions to hereditary origins of Fedra's amorous temperament, but the play lacks any sense of inevitability. Insofar as it is conceived of and understood as a drama of Christian conscience, however, it might perhaps be claimed to owe something to the ethos of Racine's supposedly Christian play.

In Proust's *A la recherche du temps perdu*, we are confronted not with imitation of Racine but with a recognised affinity. The echoes or allusions are, not surprisingly, more subtle and imaginative. Allusions are made to *Phèdre* from the start of the work and the performance in the heroine's role by the great actress Berma (generally identified with Sarah Bernhardt) is evoked more than once. But it is in the discussion of sexual jealousy in *Albertine disparue* of 1925 that that major theme in *Phèdre* is most closely examined. The narrator, Marcel, distinguishes cases in which circumstances may bring us to a sudden recognition of how much we are attached to things which we did not realise we were attached to. He believes that such cases are exemplified in the episode in which Phèdre makes her declaration of love to Hippolyte. When Hippolyte, shocked, asks whether she has forgotten that she is the wife of Thésée, she proudly rejects the suggestion:

> Et sur quoi jugez-vous que j'en perds la mémoire,
> Prince? Aurais-je perdu tout le soin de ma gloire?   (II.v.665)

(What makes you think, my lord, I have forgotten? Do you think I am no longer mindful of my good name?)

'The proof', according to Marcel, 'that "concern for her good name" is not what Phèdre is most attached to, is that she would forgive Hippolyte and snatch herself away from the counsels of Œnone, if she did not learn at that moment of Hippolyte's love for Aricie. So much is jealousy, which in love is equivalent to the loss of happiness, more keenly felt than loss of reputation. It is then that Phèdre allows Œnone to slander Hippolyte without "concerning herself to defend him", and so consigns him who wants nothing to do with her to a fate whose calamitous effects in any case offer her no consolation, since her own suicide follows closely upon his death.'

Whether Marcel's laboriously analysed reactions to the defection of Gilberte and Albertine (which no attempt has been made to summarise here) truly correspond to those of Phèdre to Hippolyte's rejection of her is open to question, but what is clear is the influence exerted by Racine's depiction of the psychology of Phèdre upon Proust's understanding of sexual jealousy. It is a matter not of formal imitation but of a shared understanding of human nature.

A remarkable modern translation of Racine's *Phèdre* is the *Phaedra* (1960) of Robert Lowell (1917–77), an American poet of patrician origins but rebellious temperament. In his preface to his translation of *Phèdre* he speaks of basing his metre on Dryden's and Pope's, but running his couplets on and avoiding inversions and alliterations. The freer rhythm of Lowell's couplets is welcome, but his frequent enjambment or running-on of lines itself becomes an obtrusive device. Lowell confesses that he inevitably echoes the style of the English Restoration, 'both in ways that are proper and in my sometimes unRacinian humour and bombast' – to which one might add a certain coarsening of tone.

In 1976, Benjamin Britten set extracts from Lowell's *Phaedra* to music to form a cantata for mezzo-soprano and small orchestra. The cantata was written for Janet Baker, who had sung the part of Phèdre in a pioneering English performance of Rameau's *Hippolyte et Aricie* under the direction of Anthony Lewis (1966). There is a marked contrast between the piteous Phèdre of Rameau and Britten's Phaedra, whose death, as Lowell's translation itself suggests, seems to raise her above her crime.

In Tony Harrison's verse tragedy, *Phaedra Britannica, after Jean Racine* (1975), Racine's Greek drama is ingeniously transmuted into an episode of British rule in India before the Mutiny of 1857, and the title alludes to the *Pax Britannica*. The play tells of the trembling of the stiff upper lip. Phèdre becomes a Memsahib; Thésée, the Governor; Hippolyte, the young Thomas Theophilus, of mixed race (reminding us that his mythical predecessor had an exotic Amazonian mother). The nurse becomes an Indian ayah, and Aricie an Indian princess. The gods of Greek mythology are replaced by those of India, standing for animal impulses, and often referred to simply as 'India'. The governor is made a brutal womaniser and a killer of animals, proud of his trophies. What disappears from this adaptation is the tragic moral conscience of Phèdre. The Indian gods are too external to the memsahib's psyche to have anything like the power of the gods in *Phèdre*. As in other modern versions of the mythical tale, the heroine's plight is a personal psychological one, rather than symbolic of the common lot of human kind, and that despite the much larger view of the meaning of the play which the playwright gives in his very interesting introduction to the published text (1976).

Racine had the advantage of working with an ancient legend which was part of his own European culture. Harrison's evocation of the Indian ambience and background is perhaps insufficiently persuasive. It permits, however, Thomas Theophilus' being destroyed by a monster while out riding, the monster being identified by an old woman as the god Siva. And there is no incongruity in the Memsahib's committing suicide by taking an exotic poison. As in Racine, she is jealous of her stepson's lover, and even the final reconciliation of the Governor with Lalamani imitates that between Thésée and Aricie in Racine, although the Governor is an altogether chillier personality than Thésée.

At the very least the play is an intellectually interesting transposition of Racine's, but it appears stilted in a way Racine's does not, despite the conventions within which Racine works. Evidently the creation of a suitable language for a modern English verse-drama poses problems. Harrison plumps for the rhyming heroic couplet, claiming to have Jean-Louis Barrault's authority or support in employing the rhythm of the iambic foot. Barrault, however, who speaks of the iambic rhythm of the human heartbeat, does not claim that the rhythms of Racine's verse are iambic. In fact he offers a most illuminating account of the flexibility of the alexandrine, showing how many kinds of metric feet can be found in it (*Mise en scène de Phèdre* (Paris 1946), pp. 41, 44–45). Harrison's very regular rhymed couplets give his lines rather snappy rhythms, quite different in effect from the dignity, gravity, and subtlety of Racine. Harrison's play is about a very different milieu from Racine's: no longer aristocratic and rarefied but rather that of a professional class closer to the concrete realities of life.

The aims of the Catalan poet and dramatist, Salvador Espriu (1913–85), in his prose drama *Una altra Fedra, si us plau* (1978) (*Another Phaedra, please*) are quite different. Espriu is a writer concerned with death and the overcoming of meaninglessness, symbolised by the myth of Ariadne and the Labyrinth. Death (Thanatos) does have a walking-on part at the end of *Una altra Fedra* – in fact, he begins by walking towards the stage audience (it is a play within a play), giving them a nasty fright, then turns and follows the protagonists into the palace – but the play otherwise has deliberately everyday qualities. The choice of play to be performed is discussed by actors in advance, and the ancient drama of Phaedra and Hippolytus is enacted before a small group of modern spectators who discuss each scene in turn, creating a certain distancing for the spectators in the theatre. The play derives manifestly from the ancient sources, and there is no Aricia, but the nurse is called Enone, and Fedra's account of her own obsession with Hipòlit is clearly indebted to Racine. She declares her passion to her stepson and, on his rejecting her, denounces him to Teseu for having designs on her. Teseu resolves the problem by sending Hipòlit back to his sporting pursuits and his hatred of Fedra. If he should find Artemis does not suffice, he should turn to Cypris (Aphrodite) prudently. It is possible to share one's life between the two goddesses. Thus tragedy is avoided pragmatically, and not without humour. Espriu is obviously concerned with the means of taming the destructive impulses within us.

Finally, a grim and powerful evocation of our social and psychical ills is offered in the *Till Fedra* (1980) (*To Phaedra*), part of a *Triptych*, not otherwise classical, published in 1981, by the Swedish dramatist Per Olov Enquist (1934–). It is a play in eight 'songs' in free verse whose quality is difficult to evaluate. Besides Fedra, Hippolytos, and Theseus, the main characters are Theramenes, Aricia and Oinone – in other words, the *dramatis personae* are, in name at least, those of Racine's play. Racine is mentioned in the author's notes, but as someone who has sold himself – or 'sold out' – like Theramenes, who figures in the play not only as Hippolytos' tutor but also as Theseus' historiographer. We remember that Racine became historiographer to Louis XIV later in the year in which *Phèdre* was produced. The gods are absent from Enquist's play, although there is some reference to the legendary ancestry of the major characters. The time and place of the action are not very clear, and the play is more or less framed by appearances of men from the cleansing department, perhaps symbolising the purity after which the classical Phaedra strove. The chief protagonists are royal but the play is conceived of as depicting middle-class life.

Fedra, the middle-aged neglected wife whose husband is away, succumbs to lust out of a sense of uselessness. There is a graphic account of her first encounter with Hippolytos, and the images of the labyrinth and the Minotaur are exploited for their erotic potential. Aricia is a rival to Fedra by virtue of her youth, but she is a frigid personality and her relationship with Hippolytos is largely political. Fedra, having declared her passion in vain to Hippolytos, accuses him of attempted rape. He is outlawed by his father, a price is put on his head and he is caught, tortured, and killed. Fedra confesses her guilt and, in order herself to avoid torture, eviscerates herself on the stage – *not* a classical ending. Enquist presents the play as a picture of a world of perverted love and affection, of the way in which a social neurosis is visible in some men's lives. The coarse eroticism of some passages forms a stark contrast with Racinian delicacy.

The play has a variety of symbolic meanings linked to particular preoccupations of the author, but it has a strong central, psychosocial concern which is distanced from the mythological or religious orientation of its classical or neo-classical predecessors. Enquist appears to have succeeded, or shown how one might succeed, in creating an effective modern tragedy on the theme of Phaedra's love for Hippolytos which does not derive its power parasitically from its antecedents in legend.

It would be idle to claim that all modern works of creative literature inspired by the legendary love of Phaedra for Hippolytus are indebted to Racine. All are inescapably debtors to Euripides and often to Seneca and Ovid. But Racine has put his own stamp on the legend and has contributed considerably to its attraction for the modern mind. He has been particularly influential in two quite different ways: in the exceptional clarity and intensity with which he has dramatised the conflict between the demands of conscience and the inflexible will of the gods; and in his perfectly achieved incorporation of the element of sexual jealousy into the plot and motivation of *Phèdre*. While the former feature gives the play its immense tragic power, the latter, although in itself almost a seventeenth-century dramatic cliché, has offered subsequent writers opportunity for dramatic inventions to which the modern audience finds it easy to respond.

Of Aristotle's two tragic emotions of pity and fear, the neo-classical writers were more at home with pity. In Racine, the hero or heroine, particularly the heroine, is often a victim, and the pathos that he or she inspires is a source of eighteenth-century sensibility. The evolution of a self-absorbed sensibility into a Romantic emotional self-indulgence, and finally into passionate rebellion against moral and religious constraints, can be traced in successive versions of the Phaedra legend. And the twentieth century has created its own images of Phaedra to embody the tensions generated in its psyche by the natural and social determinisms which beset it.

Racine's *Phèdre*, however, stands at the threshold of that age of questioning of traditional beliefs which preceded the Enlightenment, an age in which Pierre Bayle (1647–1706) was to pose with particular trenchancy the question of the compatibility of divine justice and human freedom. Although Bayle expressly dismisses pagan claims that the gods were responsible for human sinfulness (*Dictionnaire*, art. 'Hélène', rem. Y), his aporia: if all is conformable to the divine will, why must we be held responsible for our sins? defines Phèdre's anguish. For Racine and Bayle the dilemma is timeless, but Racine's timeless tragedy is the product of a particular conjuncture in time. His is the last Phaedra who can persuade us of the reality of the gods whom she holds responsible for her plight. And only *Phèdre* among neo-classical tragedies can match the poetry of Greek myth.

Further reading

Euripides and Seneca

Euripides, [Tragedies], ed. with an English translation by A. S. Way, Loeb Classical Library, 4 vols. (London and Cambridge, Massachusetts, 1912), IV

Euripides, *Hippolytos*, ed. with introduction and commentary, by W. S. Barrett (Oxford, 1964)

The Complete Greek Tragedies [in translation], ed. D. Grene and R. Lattimore, *Euripides I* (Chicago and London, 1955)

Euripides, *Ten Plays*, translated by Moses Hadas and John McLean, with an Introduction by Moses Hadas, Bantam Books (New York and Toronto, 1960)

Euripides, *Hippolytus*, A Companion with Translation by Gilbert and Sarah Lawall (Bristol Classical Press, 1986)

Seneca's Tragedies, ed. with an English translation by F. J. Miller, Loeb Classical Library, 2 vols. (London and Cambridge, Massachusetts, 1917), I

Seneca, *Phaedra*, ed. Michael Coffey and Roland Mayer (Cambridge, 1990)

Seneca's *Phaedra*, Introduction, Text, Translation and Notes by A. J. Boyle, Latin and Greek Texts (Liverpool: Francis Cairns, 1987)

Seneca, *The Tragedies, I*, translated by D. R. Slavitt (Baltimore and London 1992)

Seneca, *Four Tragedies and Octavia*, translated with an Introduction by E. F. Watling, Penguin Classics (Harmondsworth, 1966)

Racine: editions

Œuvres, ed. Paul Mesnard, Les Grands Ecrivains de la France, 8 vols., 2 albums (Paris, 1865–73)

Œuvres complètes, ed. R. Picard, Bibliothèque de la Pléiade, 2 vols. (1950) (Paris, 1964, 1966)

Théâtre complet, ed. J. Morel and A. Viala, Classiques Garnier (Paris, 1980)

Œuvres complètes, Préface de P. Clarac, L'Intégrale (Paris, 1962)

Andromache, Britannicus, Berenice, translated by J. Cairncross, Penguin Classics (Harmondsworth, 1967)

Iphigenia, Phaedra, Athaliah, translated by J. Cairncross, Penguin
   Classics (Harmondsworth, 1963)
Phèdre, ed. R. C. Knight (Manchester, 1943)
Phèdre, ed. P. Drouillard and D. A. Canal, Classiques Larousse
   (Paris, 1990)
Phèdre, ed. X. Darcos, Classiques Hachette (Paris, 1991)

Racine: background

Adam, A., *Histoire de la littérature française au XVIIe siècle,* 5 vols.
   (Paris, 1948–56), IV
Barnwell, H. T. (ed.), *Pierre Corneille. Writings on the theatre*
   (Oxford, 1965)
Bénichou, P., *Morales du grand siècle* (Paris, 1948) Collection 'Idées'
   (Paris, 1976)
Bongiorno, A., *Castelvetro on the Art of Poetry. An Abridged Trans-
   lation, with Introduction and Notes,* Medieval and Renaissance
   Texts and Studies (Binghampton, New York, 1984)
Bray, R., *La Formation de la doctrine classique en France* (1927)
   (Paris, 1957)
Brereton, G., *French Tragic Drama in the Sixteenth and Seventeenth
   Centuries* (London, 1973)
Briggs, R., *Early Modern France 1560–1715,* OPUS (Oxford, 1977)
Cave, T., *Recognitions. A Study in Poetics* (Oxford, 1990)
Cruickshank, J. (ed.), *French Literature and its Background, 2 The
   Seventeenth Century* (Oxford, 1969)
Girdlestone, C., *Jean-Philippe Rameau: his Life and Work* (1957)
   (London, 1969)
   *La Tragédie en musique (1673–1750) considérée comme genre littér-
   aire* (Geneva, 1972)
Gossip, C. J., *An Introduction to French Classical Tragedy* (London,
   1981)
Lancaster, H. C., *A History of French Dramatic Literature in the
   Seventeenth Century,* 9 vols. (Baltimore, 1929–42)
Lough, J., *An Introduction to Seventeenth-Century France* (London,
   1954)
   *Paris Theatre Audiences in the Seventeenth and Eighteenth Cen-
   turies* (London, 1957)
   Seventeenth-Century French Drama: The Background (Oxford,
   1979)
Moore, W. G., *The Classical Drama of France,* OPUS (Oxford, 1971)
Morel, J., *La Tragédie* (Paris, 1964)
*Recueil général des opéras représentés par l'Académie royale de
   musique depuis son rétablissement* (1703–45), Slatkine Reprints, 3
   vols. (Geneva, 1971)
Schérer, J., *La Dramaturgie classique en France* (Paris, 1950)

Stoye, J., *Europe Unfolding 1648–1688*, The Fontana History of Europe (London, 1969)

Truchet, J., *La Tragédie classique en France* (Paris, 1975)

Yarrow, P. J., *A Literary History of France*, II *The Seventeenth Century* (London, 1967)

Racine: general

Barnwell, H. T., *The Tragic Drama of Corneille and Racine. An Old Parallel Revisited* (Oxford, 1982)

Barthes, R., *Sur Racine* (1960) (Paris, 1963)

Bonzon, A., *La Nouvelle Critique et Racine* (Paris, 1970)

Brereton, G., *Racine. A Critical Biography* (London, 1951)

Butler, P. F., *Classicisme et baroque dans l'œuvre de Racine* (1959) (Paris, 1971)

  Racine. A Study (London, 1974)

Delcroix, M., *Le Sacré dans les tragédies profanes de Racine* (Paris, 1970)

Forman, E. (ed.), *Racine. Appraisal and Reappraisal* (Bristol, 1991)

France, P., *Racine's Rhetoric* (Oxford, 1965)

Goldmann, L., *Le Dieu caché. Etude sur la vision tragique dans les 'Pensées' de Pascal et dans le théâtre de Racine* (Paris, 1955); translated by Philip Thody as *The Hidden God* (London, 1964)

  Racine (1956) (Paris, 1970)

Hawcroft, M., *Word As Action. Racine, Rhetoric, and Theatrical Language* (Oxford, 1992)

Hubert, J. D., *Essai d'exégèse racinienne* (Paris, 1956)

Knight, R. C., *Racine et la Grèce* (1950) (Paris, 1974)

  (ed.), *Racine. Modern Judgements* (London, 1969)

Lapp, J. C., *Aspects of Racinian Tragedy* (Toronto, 1955)

Maskell, D., *Racine. A Theatrical Reading* (Oxford, 1991)

Maulnier, T., *Racine* (Paris, 1936)

Mauron, C., *L'Inconscient dans l'œuvre et la vie de Racine* (Paris, 1969)

May, G., *Tragédie cornélienne, tragédie racinienne* (Urbana: University of Illinois Press, 1948)

Moreau, P., *Racine, l'homme et l'œuvre* (1943) (Paris, 1952)

Mourgues, O. de, *Racine or, The Triumph of Relevance* (Cambridge, 1967)

Newton, W., *Le Thème de Phèdre et d'Hippolyte dans la littérature française* (Paris, 1939)

Niderst, A., *Les Tragédies de Racine* (Paris, 1975)

  Racine et la tragédie classique, 'Que sais-je?' (Paris, 1978)

Picard, R., *La Carrière de J. Racine* (Paris, 1956)

Pocock, G., *Corneille and Racine. Problems of Tragic Form* (Cambridge, 1973)

Pommier, J., *Aspects de Racine* (Paris, 1954)
Roubine, J.-J., *Lectures de Racine* (Paris, 1971)
Tobin, R. W., *Racine and Seneca* (Chapel Hill, 1971)
Venesoen, C., *Jean Racine et le procès de la culpabilité* (Paris, 1981)
Vinaver, E., *Racine. Principes de la tragédie en marge de la Poétique d'Aristote* (Manchester, 1944)
  Racine et la poésie tragique (1951) (Paris, 1963); translated by P. M. Jones as *Racine and Poetic Tragedy* (Manchester, 1955)
Weinberg, B., *The Art of Jean Racine* (Chicago and London, 1963)

Racine: Phèdre

Barrault, J.-L., *Mise en scène de 'Phèdre'* (Paris, 1946)
Croquette, B., *Racine. Phèdre*, Collection Textes et Prétextes (Paris, 1988)
Dédéyan, C., *Racine et sa 'Phèdre'* (1956) (Paris, 1978)
Mathé, R. and Couprié, C., *Phèdre, Racine*, Profil d'une œuvre (Paris, 1988)
Maulnier, T., *Lecture de 'Phèdre'* (1943) (Paris, 1967)
Mauron, C., *Phèdre* (Paris, 1968)
Puzin, C., *Phèdre. Jean Racine*, Balises (Paris, 1990)
Roubine, J.-J., *Phèdre de Racine*, Lectoguide (Paris, 1979)
Short, P., *Phèdre*, Critical guides to French texts (London, 1983)
Spitzer, L., 'The "Récit de Théramène"', in *Linguistics and Literary History* (1948) (Princeton, 1967). (This is a much more wide-ranging essay than its title suggests.)